Railways' Strangest Journeys

D0582961

Railways' Strangest Journeys

Curious and colourful journeys
from over 150 years
of rail travel

TOM QUINN

ROBSON BOOKS

First published in Great Britain in 2003 by Robson Books, The Chrysalis Building, Bramley Road, London, W10 6SP

An imprint of Chrysalis Books Group

British Library Cataloguing in Publication Data
A catalogue record for this title is available from the British Library.

ISBN 1 86105 679 6

Typeset by FiSH Books, London WC1
Printed in Great Britain by Creative Print & Design (Wales), Ebbw Vale

Contents

ACKNOWLEDGEMENTS

A number of people helped point me in the direction of dusty archives, rare books and long-vanished newspapers and magazines – without their assistance some of the best stories in this book would not have seen the light of day. Bill Wycherley let me dig through his collection of railway ephemera; Richard Westall allowed me to take over his attic for a week; Alf Lloyd sent me some hilarious stories based on personal memories and Jo Davis of the Wimbledon Wheeltappers and Shunters Historical Society got me out of a sticky corner on several occasions.

'I consider,' said Mr Weller, 'that the rail is unconstitootional and an inwasion o' priwileges...'
Charles Dickens, *Master Humphrey's Clock*
(1840)

DOG TIRED

ENGLAND, 1817

Sir Wilfred Lawson, Chairman of the Maryport and Carlisle Railway, told a remarkable – and amusing – story at one of the half-yearly meetings of his company, to illustrate the great improvement there had been in the speed of passenger trains within his lifetime.

Sir Wilfred's story concerned an old farmer who turned up with his dog at Carlisle to go by train to Wigton. The guard, on seeing the dog, went to the farmer to ask him if he had obtained a ticket for the dog.

'No,' said the farmer, 'I have got no ticket, and I'm damned if I'm going to pay for the dog.'

'In that case,' said the guard, 'the dog can't go in the train, as strict orders have been received that all dogs are in future to be paid for.'

Another farmer standing by heard the conversation, and at once suggested that the owner of the dog should tie it to the last carriage and let it run after the train. Today such a suggestion would quite rightly be greeted with horror, but this was in the very early days of the railway when people invariably underestimated the power of the new steam engines. This was also a time, of course, when animals received absolutely no protection under the law.

Anyway, the old farmer then took a piece of string out of his pocket, tied it round the dog's neck, and at once hitched it to the coupling of the van at the rear of the train. The guard, seeing what had been done, went to tell the engine driver, and asked him to drive at full speed, and so run the dog off its feet – very cruel, but the railwayman was furious at the attempt to get round the rules.

When the train arrived at the first station, ten miles down the line, the guard went to look at the dog, expecting to find it hanging by the neck dead. But, to his surprise, he found it was all right, and seemed to be enjoying the fun.

The guard went again to the driver and told him the dog had not turned a hair, and evidently had no difficulty in keeping up with the train. By this time the honour of the railway was at stake and the guard and driver were determined that they would outrun the dog even if it cost the poor dog its life.

The fireman stirred up the fire and put on more fuel till the firebox seemed to glow white hot to the very doors, and the engine went snorting and puffing and roaring along. In fact, it was going so fast that the driver became concerned that there might be an explosion or breakdown.

On arrival at Wigton station, instead of finding the poor dog hanging by the neck at least exhausted, but more probably dead, the railwaymen were surprised and furious to find the dog had broken the string and had run on in front of the train, and was standing on the platform with the string round its neck and awaiting its master's arrival.

STEAM TRIALS

ENGLAND, 1819

When virtually every inch of Durham and Northumberland was given over to coal mining, the problem of getting the coal out of the pits produced the idea of carriages or wagons on fixed rails long before Stephenson's *Rocket* made rail travel something that we would recognise today. The mine owners first attempted to use a steam-driven engine to drag their carts and carriages along the rails just after the turn of the eighteenth century.

Trials continued for the first decade of the new century and the new system was welcomed everywhere as a marvellous improvement. When steam power reached one particular pit it was greeted with such excitement that the mine owners, their friends and local dignitaries gathered to watch the first load of coal hauled from beneath the ground. But, as they watched that first train load of coal puff its way up the track, their enthusiasm quickly turned to terror – as the engine reached the assembled crowd it erupted in a huge fireball! This was no ordinary explosion – shards of metal ricocheted in every direction while lumps of coal sped away from the core of the blast like deadly missiles. Dozens were injured and, when the dust settled after that short fateful journey, thirteen lay dead, including several of the mine owners.

MAJOR OPENING

ENGLAND, 1825

Railway opening ceremonies were always extraordinary events, but perhaps the most extraordinary of all was the opening of the Stockton and Darlington Railway in 1825. The event was considered of such importance that all the inhabitants of both Stockton and Darlington were given the day off work. A programme of the planned procession was published by the directors of the company and was widely distributed. It included details of the exact times that the train would pass certain points along the route.

The order on leaving Doncaster was as follows: first came locomotive No. 1, driven by the great George Stephenson himself and after it six wagons loaded with coal and flour, then a covered wagon containing the directors, next came 21 coal wagons filled up with temporary seats for passengers and finally six more wagons loaded with coal.

A man on a horse carrying a huge flag, with the motto of the company inscribed on it, headed the procession by trotting right in front of the moving train.

The procession had enormous difficulty starting because huge crowds swarmed across the line, but, once clear of this, Stephenson put his engine to the test and reached what the passengers later described as the terrifying speed of 12 miles per hour. The horseman with the flag was at last overtaken and dropped out of the procession.

On arrival at Darlington the whole town was present to greet the intrepid travellers. Many people had viewed the journey as such a hazard-filled enterprise that they had confidently predicted that those on the train would not survive the journey.

But they did arrive safely and the procession was then rearranged; more wagons were added until the engine was pulling a total of 150 passengers as well as a large brass band. When the train arrived back at Doncaster the band, passengers and railway officials formed up in procession and marched to the town hall where a huge dinner wound up the proceedings.

In effect, this day marked the beginning of the railway, a mode of travel that, within fifty years, had spread across Europe and America and penetrated into some of the most remote corners of the world, transforming people's lives forever.

FLOATING LINE

ENGLAND, 1825

Perhaps the most extraordinary railway line ever to have existed – in terms at least of the materials used to build it – was the Durango line in Mexico. Throughout its length the ballast was made from silver ore, the sleepers from ebony. In the UK, perhaps the most remarkable line was that built by George Stephenson over Chat Moss, a huge peat bog 12 miles square and 30 feet deep that had to be crossed in order that the Liverpool–Manchester line could be completed.

Every engineer said that the track could not be laid across the moor – it was simply impossible. But being one of the most stubborn men who ever lived – not to mention the fact that he was absolutely convinced of his own abilities – Stephenson refused to accept that it could not be done. He decided to build a floating trackway. He put a thick layer of broom and heather on the surface of the bog and overlaid it with brushwood and wooden hurdles. Layer upon layer was added until the soggy quagmire could take no more. On this dense brushwood raft temporary sleepers were laid. The work was slow and incredibly expensive and laborious because every ounce of material had to be brought to the site in trucks pushed along the track manually.

Once the sleepers were in position on the floating raft the spaces between them were stuffed with heather rather than ballast and tar barrels were laid end to end along the length of the track and down at the sides of the raft to act as a drain.

The most difficult part of the job was joining the floating line to the solid sections at either end of the moor. At the Manchester

6

end, tens of thousands of tons of gravel were poured into the seemingly bottomless pit of the moor. All of it vanished and again the experts told Stephenson it could not be done. He, however, refused to give up and, month after month, the gravel continued to be poured into the moss. At last, the gravel bank rose out of the waters and the track connection could be made. Those who travelled on that early line would hardly have realised that they were enjoying one of the world's most remarkable railway journeys on Stephenson's floating roadway.

STEPHENSON CROSS-EXAMINED

ENGLAND, 1827

Just how extraordinary the whole idea of rail travel once seemed can be judged by a remarkable exchange between the great railway pioneer George Stephenson and a parliamentary commission. Stephenson was examined by a commission that was openly hostile to the whole theory and practice of rail travel. They believed that neither men nor materials were capable of withstanding the terrible shocks and strains of high-speed travel – by high speed they meant 12 miles an hour. So the commission was entirely bent on discovering the terrible dangers of railway travel from the man who was said to know most about it, namely George Stephenson, the father of the railway and one of the greatest engineers of the age.

One highly sceptical barrister who was entirely ignorant of anything to do with engineering opened the questioning: 'Of course, when a body is moving upon a road, the greater the velocity the greater the momentum that is generated?'

'Certainly,' came Stephenson's reply.

'What would be the momentum of 40 tons moving at the rate of 12 miles an hour?'

'It would be very great.'

'Have you seen a railroad that would stand that?'

'Yes.'

'Where?'

'Any railroad that would bear going 4 miles an hour; I mean to say that if it would bear the weight at 4 miles an hour, it would bear it at 12.'

'Taking it at 4 miles an hour, do you mean to say that it would not require a stronger railway to carry the same weight 12 miles an hour?'

'I will give an answer to that. Every one, I dare say, has been over ice, when skating, or seen persons go over; and they know that it would bear them at a greater velocity than it would if they went slower; when it goes quickly, the weight in a manner ceases.'

'Is not that dependent upon the hypothesis that the railroad is perfect?'

'Yes; and I mean to make it perfect.'

Stephenson's great difficulty was to persuade someone with no knowledge of engineering that something that seemed to defy common sense could be true. To the untrained mind it seemed quite bizarre, not to say unbelievable, that something very heavy, like a train, travelling at great speed on metal tracks could stay upright. The questioning continued.

'Do not wrought-iron rails bend?' said the MP. 'Take Hetton Colliery, for instance.'

'They are wrought iron, but they are weak rails.'

'Do you not know that they bend?'

'Perhaps they may, not being made sufficiently strong.'

'And if made sufficiently strong, that will involve an additional expense?'

'It will.'

'You say the machine can go at the rate of 12 miles an hour. Suppose there is a turn upon the road, what will become of the machine?'

'It would go round the turn.'

'Would it not go straight forward?'

'No.'

'What is to be the height of the flange of the wheel?'

'One inch and a quarter.'

'Then if the rail bends to the extent of an inch and a quarter, it will go off the rail?'

'It cannot bend. I know it is so in practice.'

'Did you ever see 40 tons going at the rate of 12 miles an hour?'

'No; but I have seen the engine running from 8 to 10 miles round a curve.'

'What was the weight moved?'

'I think little, except the engine.'

'Do you mean to tell us that no difference is to be made between those 40 tons after the engine, and the engine itself?'

'It is scarce worth notice.'

'Then, though the engine might run round and follow the turn, do you mean to say that the weight after it would not pass off?'

'I have stated that I never saw such a weight move at that velocity; but I could see at Killingworth that the weight was following the engines, and it is a very sharp curve: it is a sharper curve there than I should ever recommend to be put on any railroad.'

'Have you known a stage-coach overturn, when making not a very sharp curve, when going very fast?'

'That is a different thing: it is top-heavy.'

'Will none of your wagons be top-heavy?'

'They will not.'

Stephenson won the day despite the commission's scepticism. And the rest, as they say, is history.

SITTING ON THE VALVE

AMERICA, 1830

The first locomotive ever built in the USA was the *Best Friend*, built by E L Miller of the West Point Foundry for the Charleston and Hanbury Railroad Company of South Carolina, in 1830. Miller faced strong opposition to his plan to start building locomotives and couldn't raise any money from investors or banks, so he used his own money and his own initiative.

Best Friend had a vertical boiler with no fire tubes and looked pretty much like a giant beer bottle, but all those who saw it were astonished by this new and marvellous machine. At a time when most people still travelled by horse and had never seen anything mechanical that was capable of travelling at speed, *Best Friend* was an extraordinary sight – but not, alas, for long.

The fact that machines were so little understood at this time led to many mishaps and occasionally a serious accident. The fate of the *Best Friend* is a case in point. The only man who really knew how it worked and who understood its limitations was the man who built it. And his explanations to his staff about how it worked, and the intricacies of its operation, must have largely fallen on deaf ears. They viewed *Best Friend* – and the reaction was the same for very early locomotives wherever and whenever they were introduced across the world – as a kind of mechanical horse. If you mistreated a horse it might kick you or, ultimately, die – but that was about the limit of possibilities. Machines – particularly iron horses – must, they thought, be the same. But of course they weren't.

Thus it happened that an inexperienced fireman on *Best Friend* was having his lunch one fine day after a long morning's stoking when his peaceful half-hour was disturbed by the noise of steam escaping from the boiler. At first he took no notice, but then the noise began to annoy him. He put up with it for a while longer and then decided it was ruining his appetite and something had to be done. But what could he do? All he'd been trained to do was stoke the firebox. Then horse mentality entered the equation. If something is making a noise that you don't like you shut its mouth – and that's exactly what he tried to do with *Best Friend*.

The noise was coming from the safety valve so the fireman sat on it and happily continued eating. Some time later there was an explosion so loud that it was heard halfway across the state. *Best Friend* was reduced to a few tangled pieces of metal and very little of the fireman was ever found. Luckily, however, very few other people were around at the time of the accident because anyone within fifty yards of the explosion would almost certainly have been killed.

SCOFFING AT A PIONEER

ENGLAND, 1830

In these days of lightning-fast express trains it is hard to realise that 150 years ago the locomotive was in its infancy, and its ultimate possibilities were not dreamed of. At that time a well-known resident of Liverpool said that if it were ever proved possible for a locomotive engine to travel at 10 miles per hour, he would eat a stewed engine-wheel for breakfast. Whether the gentleman lived long enough to enjoy this curious meal is not recorded.

The press almost universally scoffed at the same idea of rapid train travel, declaring it impossible and denouncing its advocates as lunatics and fanatics. 'Twelve miles an hour,' exclaimed the *Quarterly Review*, in 1825, 'twelve miles an hour! As well might a man be shot out of a Congreve Rocket.'

In about 1830, the great pioneering steam engineer George Stephenson was cross-examined (and not for the first time!) by a parliamentary committee, with regard to constructing a railroad from Liverpool to Manchester. The interview was recorded for posterity by a local newspaper reporter.

'Well, Mr Stephenson, perhaps you could go 17 miles an hour?'
'Yes,' was the reply.
'Perhaps some 20 miles might be reached?'
'Yes, certainly.'
'Twenty-five, I dare say, you do not think impossible?'
'Certainly not impossible.'
'Dangerous?'
'Certainly not.'

'Now, tell me, Mr Stephenson,' said the parliamentary member with indignation, 'will you say that you can go 30 miles?'

'Certainly,' was the answer, as before.

Questions ended for the time, and the wiseacres of the committee burst into a roar of laughter. But Stephenson built the road and, on his trial trip, astonished the world with a speed of 36 miles an hour.

RAIL SURVEYORS IN THE SCHOOLYARD

ENGLAND, 1831

Once parliament had taken to the idea of railways it took to them wholeheartedly. So much so, in fact, that it quickly passed some of the most remarkable legislation ever enacted. The legislation gave railway engineers and surveyors powers that made them seem at times above the law. Much of this allowed railway surveyors to go wherever they pleased. And if this meant climbing on someone's roof or traipsing through their garden or even entering the house it was allowed under the various railways acts passed in the early part of the nineteenth century.

Landowners were outraged at any invasion of their property and numerous instances are recorded of surveyors being attacked or shot at by irate landowners who believed – foolishly as it turns out – that the rights of property and the laws of trespass superseded the new laws governing the railways. They did not. Railways were the new thing and they took precedence over pretty much everything. An example of what this extraordinary situation could lead to was recorded by a London reporter who heard of a case of a schoolmaster in Camden finding the peace of his family disturbed by the announcement one Saturday morning that strange men were clambering over his garden wall. On sallying forth, indignant, to demand the reason for the intrusion, he found the men coolly engaged, with hammers and cold chisels, in boring a hole through the wall of his summer-house.

As luck would have it, the schoolmaster's house was in the way of the proposed railway. But first there had to be a survey and it was mandatory under the new laws that in order to complete the survey the schoolmaster's house and garden had to be invaded.

For the sake of convenience, the surveying party always carried a ladder. They used this at the schoolmaster's house to climb on to a flat roof behind his sitting room. On the day in question, the schoolmaster looked up to see a pair of legs descending from beneath a blue mackintosh. The owner of the legs and one or two assistants were carefully fixing a theodolite on the flat roof, and marking with penknives the exact spot occupied by each of the three legs of the instrument.

The outraged schoolmaster, thinking the law must be on his side, leapt out through the window on to the roof and the following conversation – meticulously recorded by one of the railwaymen's assistants – took place.

'Who are you, sir, and how dare you come on to my roof?'

'Sir, I am an assistant of Mr Robert Stephenson and I am engaged on a survey for the Euston Grove extension of the London and Birmingham Railway.'

'And what business have you on my premises?'

'The centre line of the railway passes exactly beneath the plumb-bob of my instrument.'

'Don't talk to me of plumb-bobs, sir; how dare you climb up there and to have the impertinence to stare in at my windows?'

'If you will have the kindness to look at this book...'

'Don't talk to me of books! I say how dare you come here.'

'That is just what I produced the book to explain, sir...'

'What on earth do you mean, sir?'

'I mean, sir, this is the Act of Parliament in virtue of which the officers of the company are authorised to enter on the properties scheduled in the book of reference for the purposes of the survey.'

'Hang the officers of the company! And the purposes of survey! And you too, sir! Once and for all, will you leave my premises directly?'

'I regret that my duty forbids me to do so, sir, but we will be as rapid in our work and give you as little annoyance as possible.'

'Then, sir, I shall instantly send for a policeman.'

'Perhaps that will be the most satisfactory course, sir. The policeman will no doubt convince you we are only doing our duty.'

A policeman was sent for and the schoolmaster arrested for impeding the rapid progress of the great invention of the age.

FIRST-HAND ACCOUNT

ENGLAND, 1832

There are very few first-hand accounts of what it felt like to travel by rail at the very dawn of the railway era. But one man – a Mr Fergusson of Woodhill, Edinburgh – described the strangeness of a mode of transport that, at the time, must have felt pretty much like space travel today. In a note written just a day or so after the events described he wrote of the journey from Manchester to Liverpool:

> We started with eight carriages attached to the engine with such imperceptible motion, that it was only when I found myself unable to read a milestone, or to distinguish the features of those who darted past in the opposite direction, that I was led to consult my watch for the rate of travelling; when I found, to my astonishment, that the next five miles were done in 15 minutes.
>
> From the powers of the locomotive engines on the railroad, goods and passengers are conveyed from Liverpool to Manchester, a distance of 32 miles, in about two hours.
>
> Among other regulations, a watchman is stationed permanently on the line every half mile to detect any stone or other dangerous impediment upon the rail. As he sees the carriages approaching, if there is a difficulty, he stops and extends his arm in sufficient time to enable the engineer to stop the train.
>
> As we bowled along, a little circumstance, more ludicrous than dangerous, occasioned a small loss of time. The hook by

which No. 2 carriage was attached to No. 1 suddenly gave way, and the engine, with one carriage only, shot off like lightning, leaving the others to follow as they best could. The alarm was, however, quickly given, the engine reversed its movement, and the whole affair was speedily adjusted.

An old coachman, who had been forced by the railway to abandon his calling forever, mustered up resolution one morning to take a trip by the railway, and, in spite of a very reasonable stock of indignation, soon felt his asperity giving way under the excitement of such a slapping pace, and, before he had proceeded far, exclaimed in ecstasy to the engineer: 'Come now, my lad, that's it, do boil up a bit of a gallop.'

FOLDING CHIMNEY

ENGLAND, 1832

When the first railways were opened in various parts of the world, local government officials inevitably tried to ensure that the launch of their railway service was bigger and better than anyone else's. Among the most extraordinary of all was the ceremony that surrounded the opening of the Leicester and Swannington Railway on 17 July 1832.

This took place with huge rejoicing, ringing of church bells, playing of bands and firing of cannon. However, during a trial run the cannon, fitted to an open carriage at the back of the train, accidentally aimed too low and narrowly missed the engine at the front. The engineers gathered around the engine said they thought a revolution had started.

But there were no further mishaps during the trial runs and the great day began with George Stephenson driving his famous *Comet* engine. Behind the engine came the directors in an open-sided carriage fitted with a tarpaulin roof. There were as yet no specially fitted seats in the carriage so the directors brought along the chairs they sat on in the railway company boardroom. After the directors came ten coal wagons fitted with planks as seating. One wagon carried a band and local dignitaries crammed into the others. The train measured 60 yards from one end to the other and almost every inch of it was covered with flags and bunting. The cannon was carried on the last wagon and it was fired as the train approached and then left each station along the route – but only after having been aimed carefully skywards!

The journey began with the chairman giving the hand signal that all was ready. Stephenson opened the regulator and the train moved forward to deafening cheers from the crowd. The canon fired, the band struck up 'God Save the King' and church bells all along the route began to be rung.

For years afterwards, local people remembered the extraordinary spectacle of the train moving through their towns and villages and across the open countryside. Nothing like this giant, breathing flag-bedecked monster had ever been seen before and among the older generation – particularly the clergy – there were mutterings about the devil's work.

Only two incidents marred the journey and they illustrate perfectly how new the whole enterprise was. Halfway through the Glenfield Tunnel the chimney of the *Comet* was broken off after it hit the roof of the tunnel. As a result the directors in the first carriage were unrecognisable when the train appeared at the other end of the tunnel – they were completely soot-blackened. The train made an impromptu stop by the side of a brook and the directors all leapt down in their best suits and top hats and paddled about in the water for twenty minutes, desperately trying to remove the worst of the dirt.

The second accident occurred when a woman who'd knelt at the side of the track to pray for deliverance from the monster was hit by a horse that was trying to keep up with the train. The rider assumed she'd get out of the way long before he reached her but she was praying so avidly that she did not see him until it was too late. She escaped with minor injuries and the incident no doubt confirmed her worst fears about this new and entirely ungodly mode of transport.

The train achieved speeds approaching twenty miles an hour before reaching its destination and a street party that lasted through the night and well into the next day.

HORSE BEATS TOM THUMB

AMERICA, 1833

About the time the English establishment was ridiculing its early railroad efforts, in America people were laughing a good deal over the race between a horse and a locomotive in which horsepower won. In those early days, Peter Cooper built the locomotive *Tom Thumb* for the Baltimore Railroad, and ran a race with a grey horse owned by two theatre managers known as Stockton and Stokes. The horse had to pull a wagon on a second, parallel track.

The story is taken up by a reporter from the local newspaper:

Away went horse and engine, the snort of the one keeping time to the puff of the other. The grey had the best of it at first, getting a quarter of a mile ahead while the engine was getting up steam. The blower whistled, the steam blew off in vapour clouds, the pace increased, the passengers shouted, the engine gained on the horse, the stick was applied to the horse, the race was neck and neck, nose to nose; then the engine passed the horse, and a great cheer hailed the victory.

But just at this moment, when the man driving the horse was about to give up, the leather band that turned the pulley that moved the blower on the locomotive engine slipped from the drum and the safety valve ceased to scream, and the engine, for want of breath, began to wheeze and pant. In vain, Mr Cooper, who was both engine driver and fireman, lacerated his hands in attempting to replace the band on the wheel; the horse gained on the machine and passed it, to his great annoyance. Although

22

the band was quickly replaced, and steam again did its best, the horse was too far ahead to be overtaken again, and came in winner of the race.

This little engine was only meant as an experiment, but it was the first American locomotive ever made.

LEADING BY EXAMPLE

ENGLAND, 1834

Charles Fox was born in 1810. His father desperately wanted him to follow in the family tradition and become a doctor, but, in 1831, his keenness for railway engineering, which was then a new profession, persuaded him to abandon medicine for a life on the railway. He left home and went to Liverpool.

Fox got a job with Fawcett, Preston & Co., before quickly moving on to work for Ericsson, who built the *Monitor* locomotive, and who was then designing one of the locomotives that competed at the celebrated Rainhill trials. On that occasion Fox drove the locomotive. She was called, appropriately enough, the *Novelty*. But for the fact that she blew a tube, she would probably have been the winner of the prize of £500 – a huge amount at the time.

For a while, Fox became obsessed by locomotive driving – which, today, may seem rather odd given that we find it hard to believe that Old Etonians and other aristocrats (Fox was certainly that) are not the most likely candidates for train driving. In fact, when the railways began, driving was seen as very much a gentleman's profession. Fox the public school-educated former medical student was then employed for a number of years on the Liverpool and Manchester Railway, a job that he adored.

But this toff on the footplate was destined for higher things.

By 1834 he was a senior engineer at work on the Watford Tunnel where he became part of one of those remarkable incidents that typify the pioneering spirit of the early railway. The tunnel was an extremely tricky enterprise from an engineering point of view and during Fox's time as the chief supervisor of the work engineers were working in very soft ground. He was so worried about the ground that, when he was ordered to go to Birmingham to take charge of another project, he asked if the move could be delayed. His request was refused and he set off for Birmingham. A few days later he received a message that the Watford Tunnel had collapsed and eleven men had been killed. He hurried back, commissioning a special train that ran at extraordinarily high speeds, and found a scene of panic and pandemonium. Fox got the men together and said to them: 'That tunnel has to be put through, cost what it will, and therefore I want you men to volunteer.'

Not one of them would do so. 'Very well,' said Fox, 'I will do it.' And with that he got into the bucket, and was just about to be lowered down the shaft when the ganger – the leading workman – shouted 'I will not see the master killed alone.'

The two were lowered into the shaft and together they finished the length through the dangerous ground, after which the rest of the men agreed to return to work.

Fox went on to design the roof over Euston Station. He also built the iron roofs at New Street Station in Birmingham, at Paddington, and at York and elsewhere. But the railway tunnel was undoubtedly his finest hour.

ROPE TRICK

ENGLAND, 1835

Railway owners were always concerned for the safety and comfort of their passengers if for no other reason than that unhappy passengers would mean a serious dent in the company's profits. The concern for safety was not always extended to the company's paid staff, however, since they already represented a dent in the company profits. They were viewed as a necessary evil – which may explain an extraordinary experiment carried out in the mid-1830s.

The 1830s were a time when accidents were common simply because railways were in their infancy and it was only when a particular kind of accident happened that the railway company began looking for ways to prevent it happening again. With no signalling, for example, trains tended to collide a little more often than was comfortable. One railway company decided that the best way to deal with the problem of collisions was to send their trains out with the engine well ahead and the carriages well behind.

It was 1835 when they first launched their scheme to achieve this. They attached the engine to the rest of the train by a rope nearly half a mile long. This meant that if there was a collision the engine driver and firemen might be injured or killed but the rest of the train would have half a mile after the accident in which to slow down, with or without (depending on whether he'd noticed anything amiss!) the help of the guard in his brake van at the back of the train. The experiment was eventually abandoned because the rope proved more of a hindrance than anything, particularly as the train attempted to negotiate curves in the track.

TRUMPET VOLUNTARY

ENGLAND, 1835

Until relatively recently, Kirby Muxloe station in Leicestershire had the front of its platforms built up with square stones that were perforated. These were the original sleepers of the Leicester and Swannington Railway, which was surveyed by George Stephenson in the early part of the nineteenth century.

Stephenson was then engaged in the construction of the Liverpool and Manchester Railway, so he had to turn the invitation to build this railway down. In his place, his son Robert, who was only 27, got the job – the first of his many great works. The sleepers were just square blocks of stone that were placed diamond-wise at short intervals under each rail.

The line started off with only one locomotive – the *Comet* – which was built in George Stephenson's works at Newcastle and sent by sea and canal to Leicester. Passengers had not been thought of as cargo – they were designed to carry coal.

But at last a passenger coach was commissioned and built and a set of tickets made of brass was issued. These were sold to travellers and then collected by the guard and returned to the stations that issued them on the return journey.

Some years after the service began the train was bowling along at a terrifying 16 miles an hour when, despite the efforts of the engine driver, the *Comet* collided with a farmer's trap. Horse and farmer were uninjured but the trap was apparently a write-off.

After the mishap, Mr Ashlen Bagster, who managed the line, asked George Stephenson if he could not fit the engine with some

27

sort of trumpet to be blown by steam to warn horses, cows and farmers' traps of the impending arrival of the iron monster. Stephenson regarded this as being within the remit of a musician and not an engineer, so a musical instrument maker in King Street, Leicester, was entrusted with the design of the steam trumpet. No doubt he tried to pitch it as melodiously as the old mail-guard's post horn, but after numerous trials during which astonished country-folk heard the fabulous blast of brass, the pressure of steam made him fall back on the cruder principle of a whistle.

A SHIP ON THE RAILS

ENGLAND, 1836

The huge success of the very earliest railways in the North of England meant that trains quickly spread across the country, including London. The earliest London service of all was the line from the City to Greenwich.

Crowds gathered in those early days to see the extraordinary breathing monster that could pull huge loads without the assistance of horses. The new method of transport was very popular with the travelling public, or at least that part of it wealthy enough to indulge in what was seen as a luxury. But, much as people admired the technology, there were many complaints about the aesthetics of the whole enterprise. The chief complaint was that somehow the engines were rather ugly. Letters were written in great numbers to the railway company asking if they could not brighten up these dismal-looking locomotives. The real problem was that the first generation to experience railways judged them against the brightly coloured mail coaches that still dominated the national transportation system.

According to the then editor of the *Railway News*, the London and Greenwich Railway (L&GR) company took the complaints about the appearance of their engines very seriously. They studied the problem and after some time came up with a solution. Because the brick-built viaducts that carried the line into London looked rather like Roman aqueducts, a bright spark at the L&GR suggested to Braithwaite and Milner, who made the company's engines, that they should build a locomotive in the style of a Roman galley.

The result was that, a year later, huge crowds gathered at Cornhill in the City to watch the arrival of a train pulled by a very passable imitation of an ancient ship.

When word got out, much of the route was regularly lined with spectators eager to see this extraordinary engine which was – as its inventor had suggested – particularly impressive when viewed from the ground as it passed sedately over one or other of the company's viaducts. The only thing that spoiled the general effect was the noise and the clouds of dense smoke.

Despite its initial popularity, the idea of locomotives imitating ships did not catch on and the London and Greenwich soon reverted to more practical-looking engines.

GUARDS ON THE ROOF

ENGLAND, 1836

The guards on branch trains had an appalling time in the earliest days of the railway. The brakes of these local trains were worked from the roof of the carriages, the guards riding outside, in an unprotected seat at the end of the carriages, and applying the brake when necessary by turning on a hand screw.

A journey from Wymondham to Dereham, in Norfolk, cured one young guard of any notion that travelling outside might be fun.

At the end of the train were two brake vans, each fitted with outside seats for the guards. The two vans had been hooked up to the train in such a way that the two outside seats faced each other over the roofs of the vans. The older, more experienced guard sat on the seat that enabled him to turn his back to the engine, while the young guard – who'd never been assigned to rooftop duties before – had the seat facing the direction in which the train would soon be travelling.

All seemed comfortable enough at first, though the iron framework of the seat was freezing. But, as the train picked up speed, the dust, smoke and steam from the engine filled the young man's eyes, ears and nose. In fact, by the time the short journey was over, he was choked and soot-blackened from head to toe and almost blinded.

The smoke and steam from the engine was directed by the wind down the tops of the carriages and straight into his face. So much dirt and smoke had gone into his lungs that he could not speak or walk. He had to be carried down from his high perch and it took two hours for him to recover sufficiently to return to his duties. The older guard later told his younger colleague that the trick was to wear a thick muffler and wrap it well round the head and under no circumstances should he look up or attempt to see anything of the journey. This, of course, made travelling on the outside pretty pointless, since being able to see ahead and apply the brakes in time was the sole point of the outside seats.

After some years the extraordinary outside roof seat was fitted with a small box-shaped shelter and then a small rough curtain was added to give some protection from the weather and the worst of the smoke and steam. The open van was the next advance, whereby a vehicle would have one end covered and designed for luggage and parcels, while the other end was open and fitted with a small seat for the guard, with the brake wheel close at hand.

OUT AND ABOUT

AMERICA, 1837

A newspaper report about the opening of the Cumberland Valley Railroad in America in 1837 reported that when the first train set off:

> Dogs dropped their tails between their legs and ran like frightened fiends, howling and trembling, to the far-off mountains. Men cleared ditches and hedges at a single bound as the hissing engines approached. Old men and women leaned on their staffs and gazed in visible awe as if Domesday was at hand.

But even after the astonishment and awe had abated, ignorance about the new mode of transport continued for many years. A reporter from the same American newspaper, who talked to many local people in the months and years after the railway arrived, once overheard a farm worker and his wife chatting to each other by their garden gate. It was a warm evening, quiet and with not a breath of wind.

The reporter slowed as he heard them talking about the new and startling invention, the railway engine.

At length, the old farm labourer remarked to his wife, with an air of enormous wisdom: 'It's a fine night tonight, Maggie. I shouldn't wonder if there isn't a train or two out tonight.'

BEDS ON THE TRAIN

ENGLAND, 1838

One of the biggest problems on the railway before signalling and proper fencing were established was seeing far enough ahead of the engine to apply the brakes when something had strayed on to the tracks or when the train was in danger of running into another train or stationary wagon.

To get round the problem, one railway company sent a train out with a man sitting at the front with a telescope. The trial was deemed unsatisfactory because the lookout man was instructed never to take his eye away from the telescope – in practice, fatigue and boredom made this impossible.

Other problems with early trains centred on the coupling system between carriages. When simple chains were used, the noise of clanking was indescribable whenever the train slowed down or speeded up. Worse still, passengers were thrown about as the carriages caught up with and bashed into each other. One passenger complained that he had not paid good money to be knocked about as if he were a prize fighter.

Alarmed at the damage to its reputation, the railway company announced that it had found a solution to the problem. The company's new highly comfortable train was given its first outing on a warm spring day. All the seats on the train had been sold after a sustained advertising campaign alerted passengers and local officials and dignitaries to what was described as a 'new era in travelling comfort'.

The journey was indeed far more comfortable than the passengers had dared to imagine – and how was this achieved? By the simple expedient of fitting a mattress (from a bed) to the gap between each carriage. Mattresses were also fitted at the front and back of the train to allow for bumps on the buffers.

History does not record how long the experiment lasted, but it certainly did wonders for the railway company's reputation in the short term.

EXCURSION TRAIN

ENGLAND, 1838

The first experience of the South West Railway in the matter of excursion trains was not a happy one. The line had been opened in May 1838, about a week before the Derby was due to be run, and to meet the demands of those anxious to attend what, at the time, was seen as a national festival of incalculable importance. The company announced that they would run no less than eight excursion trains.

When the great day arrived, railway officials were horrified to discover that some hours before the first train was due to start, a crowd of more than five thousand people had assembled at the departure station at Nine Elms in south London.

Trains were prepared and despatched as fast as humanly possible but the crowd increased much faster than the railway could carry them away. The crowd was so vast that the station closed at ten o'clock to keep them out, lest it be swamped, but by this time the mob had got completely out of hand – they broke down the gates and charged the platforms!

A train that had been chartered for a private party was hijacked, its wealthy passengers summarily ejected and the driver told in no uncertain terms that he must set off.

As soon as the train had left the station, to a huge cheer from the mob, the police were called and the rest of the mob was scattered by horses and truncheon-wielding police officers. It was a scene of indescribable chaos – half the station fencing had been crushed, a platform branch of Smiths the newsagents looted, posters and railway timetables defaced. Railway company officials were so shaken by the day's events that they closed that station and refused to open it again for three days.

AMATEURS

ENGLAND, 1838

Until appropriate legislation was passed, individuals regularly put their own trains on the railway company tracks if they fancied themselves as train drivers.

In the early and mid-1830s a certain Dr Dionysius Lardner had become addicted to doing this. He had his own locomotive engine but nowhere to run it. His solution was to take his partly dismantled engine to the local railway company tracks on the back of several large carts. He and his assistants would then assemble the engine, load it with coal and water and Lardner would set off down the tracks.

There was so little traffic in the 1830s that he got away with this dozens of times, despite the fact that the owners of the line were never informed. Then, towards the end of the decade, Lardner came unstuck. It was a bright clear day and he set off in the usual way. He was enjoying himself enormously and had built up a good head of steam when – not realising that he was actually driving up the down line – he ran into the 8.15 express. The noise of the two engines hitting each other could be heard across the county, but by a miracle no one was killed. Three passengers were slightly injured and both Lardner's engine and the company's train were badly damaged. Lardner, a notorious eccentric, was furious with the company for having their train in the wrong place at the wrong time! Despite the damage he'd caused, Lardner could not be prosecuted. As a result of his actions a change in the law was deemed necessary and the private use of railway lines came to an end.

STATIONARY ENGINE

ENGLAND, 1838

For a long time restrictions were placed on the development of the railway for reasons that now seem either charming or insane or both. All trains entering London from the North were, for example, forbidden to move under steam from Camden Town to the main stations at St Pancras and King's Cross.

It was argued that allowing the trains to make the last part of the journey in the normal way, through such a densely populated region, would cause babies to be born prematurely, horses to run wild and old people to die before their time. There was also the practical consideration that no early locomotive could pull the trains up the steep gradients out of the big London termini.

The solution was quickly found and on the day the first train arrived at Camden Town from the north its engine was uncoupled and it was attached to a rope. The rope ran off down the rail to a fixed engine standing ready at King's Cross.

A primitive form of telegraph signal was then used by the Camden Town official to tell the man in charge of the fixed engine at King's Cross that it was time to pull the train in.

Even more extraordinary was that when the train had been pulled in as far as possible, passengers discovered they were still 200 yards short of the platform where they hoped to alight.

With the rope untied, the last part of the train's journey was completed courtesy of a huge gang of porters and railway police who quite literally pushed the train into its proper position at the side of the platform.

CAVALIER ATTITUDE

ENGLAND, 1839

For the first twenty years that railway travel was possible accidents were frequent rather than serious. They were frequent because people treated the railway as if it were a toy or a harmless novelty; they were not always as serious as they were one hundred years later, simply because 20 miles per hour was as fast as they could go.

Locomotive engines were looked upon as a kind of fairground attraction and it was not until the casualty list began to lengthen that the railway staff and the general public learned to treat them with respect and caution. The slogan 'Safety First' did not become the watchword for the railway for many years.

Every week there would be instances of passengers jumping off trains that were travelling at full speed – people who'd known only travel by horse and carriage simply could not imagine that travelling at 20 miles an hour rather than 6 or 7 called for an entirely different kind of attitude.

Railway records for the 1830s are filled with entries such as the following:

> Injured, jumped out after his hat. Fell off while riding on the side of a wagon. Skull broken while riding on top of a carriage and coming into collision with a bridge. Guard's head struck against a bridge when attempting to move a passenger who had improperly seated himself outside.

'Of the serious accidents reported to the Board of Trade,' writes one authority, '22 happened to persons who jumped off when the carriages were going at speed, generally after their hats, and five persons were run over when lying drunk or asleep upon the line.'

The cavalier attitude to the dangers of the railway can perhaps best be summed up in the amusing report of what could have been a fatal accident on the Great North Railway. A wealthy landowner who'd decided to take a Sunday afternoon stroll along the railway line in 1839 was hit by a locomotive and hurled down the embankment. On being picked up he simply said: 'If I've damaged the engine I'm quite happy to pay for it.'

MUSCULAR ENGINE

ENGLAND, 1839

In the 1830s, when the railway was still young and thrilling, neither the public nor the specialists were convinced that the right system – namely steam – had been hit upon. The fact that power that did not involve the horse had been discovered seems to have inspired all kinds of ideas for new-fangled and often outlandish modes of transport. One reputable railwayman suggested a 'patent aerial steam carriage which is to convey passengers, goods, and despatches through the air, performing the journey between London and India in four days, and travelling at the rate of 75 to 100 miles per hour.' All kinds of substitutes for locomotives on the ground were also eagerly sought.

The Globe newspaper reported that a 'professional gentleman at Hammersmith had invented an entirely new system of railway carriage, which may be propelled without the aid of steam at an extraordinary speed, exceeding 60 miles an hour'. No details were given.

Another writer said of the Edinburgh and Glasgow Railway that it had:

> The discernment to employ a Mr Davidson, a gentleman of much practical knowledge and talent, to construct for them an electro-magnetic carriage. The carriage, 16 feet long by 7 feet wide, was duly placed upon the rails, and propelled by eight powerful electro-magnets about a mile and a half along the railway, travelling at the rate of upwards of four miles an hour,

a rate that might be increased by giving greater power to the batteries, and enlarging the diameter of the wheels.

This bizarre contrivance was described as a 'far more valuable source of power than that clumsy, dangerous, and costly machine the steam-engine'.

But perhaps the most extraordinary alternative to steam power was tested in 1839. The patent office records for that year mention two gentlemen known as Taylor and Couder who registered an ingenious system by which a carriage was to be drawn along the line 'by the muscular power of the two guards who constantly accompany it'.

The carriage was described as very light and elegant in appearance, and capable of carrying seven or eight passengers at a speed of 18 miles per hour. 'We have no doubt,' records a railway newspaper, 'that these machines will come into general use, as they will effect considerable saving to the company in time, trouble and expense of running an engine'.

When there was an attempt to test the new carriage no two guards of sufficient muscular ability to move the thing an inch could be found and the idea died even as it was born.

NEVER BELIEVE THE PAPERS

IRELAND, 1840

The railway engineer Charles Fox, who designed a number of stations and had been a locomotive driver in his youth, once found himself working on a railway in Ireland. The company for which he worked had fixed a day for the opening of their new railway, notwithstanding a warning given by one of the contractors involved in building the track, that he would not allow the opening to take place until he'd been paid.

Railway companies were often strapped for cash, even during the railway building boom, and there had been too many financial collapses for suppliers ever to feel entirely happy about the companies that bought their goods and expertise.

The company ignored the contractor, invited the mayor of the city to start the train, had a battery of artillery fire a salute just before it left the station, and filled the special train with their friends, intending to take them to the other end of the railway, some twenty miles away, where a luncheon was awaiting them.

The mayor waved his green silk flag, the band struck up, the artillery fired a salute (bringing down the whole of the station's glass roof), and the train started, only to be brought to a standstill within a few hundred yards by a man on the line waving his arms and shouting that the rock cutting had fallen in. In fact, several hundred tons of rock had been blown on to the track about a mile ahead by a gunpowder blast, thus effectively blocking the line and rendering it impossible for the train to proceed.

The chairman of the railway company was so furious that for a time he became completely unhinged – he called in the militia and tried to have everyone concerned with building and maintaining his railway arrested. Even his friends sitting patiently in the open carriages of the stalled train became nervous as he ranted and raved, and eventually crept away as inconspicuously as they could. Only the navvies benefited from the disaster – the railway owner thought they were too unimportant to be arrested and, since the VIPs couldn't get to their vast and luxurious lunch, the navvies ate it instead.

Late in the afternoon it was remembered that a full account of the glorious opening, the splendid 20-mile ride at top speed and the vastly amusing speeches, had already been sent to the newspapers. There was a flurry of activity as various secretaries and other officials fired off telegrams to the newspaper in an attempt to stop the story being printed, but the answer came back: 'Too late – gone to press', the result being that a full account of the glorious journey and concluding ceremony appeared in the papers the next day in Dublin. Despite none of it having taken place.

HOLIDAY OUTING

ENGLAND, 1840

In these days when holiday travel by road, rail and air is commonplace, it is difficult to imagine a time when the idea of any kind of holiday was a new and extraordinarily exciting innovation. The first great era of holiday travel for ordinary people centred on the excursion train and it is impossible now to imagine how momentous the prospect of such an outing must once have seemed. Some idea of the excursion's importance in the popular imagination can be gleaned from the fact that for the first ten years that excursion trains existed their journeys were always reported at length in local and national newspapers.

The very first excursion train ran from Nottingham to Leicester on 20 July 1840. Half-fare tickets were issued for all (and this became standard practice for all excursion trains) but the demand was so enormous – ten thousand people applied for three hundred tickets – that the company realised it had found a winning formula and began to run excursion trains every week.

Trains became longer and longer as the railway companies added more and more carriages to carry the seemingly endless stream of passengers. Since they were all in no hurry it didn't matter that these vastly over-extended trains travelled at half the normal speed of a regular train on the same route.

On one unforgettable day in August 1840 an excursion train from Nottingham to Leicester carried no fewer than 2,400 passengers. A journalist from the *Leicester Mercury* described the remarkable scene:

The engines were massively overloaded and progress was slow. Then, at about 12.30, a white flag was seen at the station waving in the air. The enormous train – nearly 80 carriages in all – began to groan.

The railway company's biggest locomotive standing majestically at the head of the unbelievably long train seemed almost to brace itself for the impossible task ahead of it. There was a visible shudder as it took up the strain, leaned into the task and tried to move the impossibly huge load.

For a second, it looked as if this excursion was going nowhere. Then at last, after much clanking and blowing, the vast edifice began, inch by inch, to move. It was as if some inconceivably huge monster had come to life. The train had covered several miles before it reached its maximum speed of ten miles an hour.

The driver and guard had been warned that the train was so heavy it might not stop in time at the other end of the journey unless they took special precautions. Special precautions in the event took the form of waiting until the lumbering giant had reached its top speed – ten miles an hour – and then immediately beginning to apply the brakes. The tactic was successful; and at a snail's pace the longest excursion train in the history of the world pulled gently into Leicester station.

EFFICIENT COMMUNICATION

ENGLAND, 1840

One of many Victorian railway acts stipulated that there had to be an efficient means of communication between passengers and, to quote from the original draft legislation, 'the servants of the company on every passenger train running for more than 20 miles without stopping'.

The public demand for this had been increasing for several years prior to the change in the rules, and a private member's bill to enforce it had passed the Commons in 1867 but was defeated in the Lords.

All the railway companies were opposed to the change, the Great Western chairman being particularly prominent in its dissent. He considered such a thing 'quite uncalled for and likely to cause more accidents, by the stoppage of trains at unexpected places, than it could possibly prevent'.

Apart from such opposition as this, the difficulty was to find an efficient and relatively inexpensive form of communication. Innumerable plans were proposed, mechanical, electric and pneumatic, and many of them tried out, but none were found satisfactory.

For a short while there was a plan to employ a man to constantly walk up and down the length of the train peering into the carriages, but in the absence of corridor trains this was always going to be difficult. His sole responsibility in the event of a problem would be to run to the carriage nearest the engine and then speak to the driver through a tube. Another idea put forward as a serious suggestion was that two vacuum tubes should be fitted and a message headed 'Emergency: Stop the Train' would be inserted in each. One message would hurtle back to the guard's van, the other forward to the engine.

Perhaps the wackiest idea was that pulling the emergency cord would release several specially trained pigeons secured in nesting boxes on the outside of the train. The birds would fly to the engine and land in the cab, telling the driver something was amiss. The idea was tried in 1840 and was only dropped when someone pointed out that the released pigeon would not be able to keep up with the speeding train!

A more realistic trial involved running a cord along the eaves of the carriages from a wheel and bell in the rear guard's van to the whistle. Then a gong fitted to the engine and attached to a cord was tried. This was approved by the Board of Trade and generally adopted right across the railway system until the turn of the nineteenth century.

LEFT BEHIND

ENGLAND, 1840

For many years after the railway became an accepted means of travel, elderly aristocrats who'd grown up in the coaching days got round the problem of hating these new-fangled trains but loving arriving at their destination quickly by loading their old horse-drawn carriages on to an open freight wagon. They would then sit in the privacy of their carriages and get to London, or wherever, at top speed but in a style consistent with their sense of what was befitting their station.

One elderly lord tried this on the London to Brighton line. All went well until the train reached the Balcombe Tunnel. Halfway through the long unlit route through the hill the wagon on which the old man's carriage was fastened, which was the last vehicle, became disengaged from the rest of the train. The unfortunate occupant, realising he'd been left behind, shouted for help but amid the enormous din of the tunnel he had no hope of being heard. Alone in the dark the old man was too terrified to move but, within minutes, might have been killed by the next train.

Suddenly, he heard the noise of a train approaching and began to say his prayers – but he was lucky; the engine turned out to have been sent specifically to look for him. Lord and carriage were attached to the new engine and then carried to Brighton, where they arrived soon after the train that had left them behind. The elderly lord vowed never to travel by carriage-on-train again.

THE COAL CARRIERS

ENGLAND, 1842

The idea of carrying coal by train once caused consternation, soul searching and heartache for dozens of railway directors. At a meeting in London, one director stood up and shouted: 'If we carry coal they'll be asking us to carry dung next!' So in the weeks that led up to the first shipment of coal being moved, one railway company issued strict instructions that the matter was to be treated with the utmost secrecy. If word got out that the railway was carrying coal the directors believed that passengers would desert them en masse. This bizarre idea was undoubtedly connected to the fact that rail travel was enormously fashionable in its early days and the fashionable traveller at that time was the rich traveller. There was little profit in carrying third-class passengers, but huge profits in carrying the wealthy. But would the wealthy travel by rail if they felt a trainload of coal had just preceded them down the track? The directors thought not. So, when that first shipment set off, each wagon was tied down with beautifully coloured tarpaulins, to give the impression that goods of a delicate and refined nature were being carried, rather than big lumps of sooty anthracite!

ANGRY ARISTOCRAT

ENGLAND, 1843

When the railways first began to spread across England, the engineers who surveyed the land and marked out the route the iron road was to take made full use of the extraordinary powers parliament had only recently granted them. Never before had the establishment – particularly the most powerful segment of the establishment, the landed aristocracy – been put in a position in which their rights were seen as secondary to the rights of commercial enterprise.

But the government and business leaders knew that the railway was the future, that the railway meant increased efficiency on a scale never before dreamed of and profits to match. The country would prosper if railways were allowed to develop unhindered, which is why parliament gave the engineers the right to enter any and every piece of land deemed necessary for their work.

But, after centuries of having it pretty much their own way, the landed gentry were understandably outraged that their interests, for the first time ever, did not come first. Some landowners set their keepers on the railway engineers if they caught them on their land; some tried – unsuccessfully – to sue the railway companies. Others, realising that they could not legitimately stop the surveyors and engineers, made sure that their most savage dogs were always loose whenever they heard that the railwaymen were in the area. One or two of the richest, most powerful, and most conservative took the law into their own hands.

One elderly aristocrat, who was distantly related to Queen Victoria, threatened to shoot the 'damned engine' if it crossed his land. For months he had to be restrained from attacking the engineers who laid tracks across his land and, when the first train came through, he stood at the edge of the line and fired both barrels of his shotgun at the locomotive. Amid the noise and steam of the engine itself no one noticed, but the next time the train came through the old man fired at the engine and at the first carriage narrowly missing the passengers. He was subsequently arrested and bound over to keep the peace. For such a serious offence anyone else would have been transported to New South Wales or, at the very least, locked away in Newgate Prison for a decade or so. But the elderly aristocrat was a relative of the Queen and prison was therefore out of the question.

Months passed after the second of the two shotgun incidents and the railway companies assumed that the old man had got used to the change that had come about. But then an odd-looking character began to be seen regularly on the local trains. He had the general appearance of a working man, with thick homespun clothes very much the worse for wear, heavy clogs and a workman's pack. But at a time when few working men travelled by train because it was so expensive his regular trips seemed very much out of keeping with his status.

Then one day he was seen behaving very oddly just moments before the train was derailed. No one was injured but the locomotive and carriages were badly damaged together with a substantial stretch of the track. The derailment happened on the old aristocrat's land and, within minutes of it happening, dozens of workmen appeared, as if from nowhere, and, having assured the driver and guard that they were from the railway company, proceeded to rip up several hundred yards of track, on the grounds that it was too badly damaged now and would have to be replaced anyway. The driver and guard were too shaken to object and by the time senior railway officers arrived on the scene both the track and the workmen who'd ripped it up had disappeared.

The old workman, with his fustian clothes, was never again seen on the train and the cause of the derailment was never discovered – all the evidence that might have been revealed by an examination of the tracks had vanished, along with the tracks themselves. The whole incident remained a mystery, but rumours persisted in the area that the old working man had in fact been the landowner in disguise and that somehow he'd managed to travel on the train and derail it just as it crossed his land. These suspicions were never proved but curiously a few months after the incident the old landowner retreated to his estates in Scotland and, as far as anyone knew, he never returned to England.

ONE MAN'S STATION

ENGLAND, 1844

As the railway gradually spread across the land in the 1830s and 1840s, the men who ran it became increasingly aware of their powers. Parliament rarely said no to the demands of these new high-powered entrepreneurs; if old buildings needed to be demolished to make way for the iron road parliament usually rushed through the necessary legislation. Progress was the watchword and, since the railway was believed to be the future, the demands of the railwaymen had to take precedence over everything else. It is certainly true that deference to Queen Victoria was such that when, for example, she demanded that the railway be routed well away from Windsor Castle, that is what happened. Queen Victoria could dictate to the railway but few others would dare – with one exception.

In the 1840s, the quiet green countryside of Middlesex, some six miles from the City of London, had yet to be transformed into the endless urban sprawl we see today. When the railway first crossed this part of the countryside on its way from London to Harrow there was no need for a new station on Acton Lane, which ran northwards across thinly populated fields from the village of Chiswick. But the railway manager lived on lonely Acton Lane and he needed to catch the train pretty regularly.

Which is why *Bradshaw's Guide* for May 1844 shows a new station open on the London and North Western Railway called Willesden. Prior to this there was no stop between London and Harrow. Willesden station, six miles from London, and Sudbury station, were opened on the same day, together with those at Pinner and Bushey. Willesden was a small roadside station on Acton Lane, but it was fully equipped with a coal fire-heated waiting room, elaborate shelters and beautifully kept flowerbeds. Local people were baffled – why on earth build a station where so few people lived? The answer was simple: it was built entirely for the convenience of Captain Huish, the railway manager who lived nearby.

KEEP ON WORKING

ENGLAND, 1845

The Irish and Scots, mostly poor people from remote rural areas or from urban slums, built most of Britain's canal infrastructure and, of course, its railways. When everything had to be dug, cut, covered, built and demolished by hand, a huge number of hands were needed and the strength and endurance of navvies was legendary. It was estimated towards the end of the nineteenth century that the railroads of Britain cost £1,000 (at least £200,000 in today's money) a mile just in beer for the navvies.

One of the most extraordinary stories about the railway navvy was centred on the tunnel at Bugsworth in Derbyshire, just north of Chinley, when the Midland Railway was being created back in the 1840s. The mouth of the tunnel fell in, and a small gang of navvies were entombed. A short rescue shaft was quickly sunk, but it still took a day and a night to reach the buried men. They were found lying, almost dying, exhausted for want of air, and on the floor their last candle was flickering, and in a few minutes would have gone out.

The rescue was just in time, but when the men recovered they told a strange tale of one of the most prosaic of heroic deeds. They had been startled by the fall of rock – there was absolutely no warning – and in seconds they found they were completely shut in. Their leader said that initially they were afraid but quickly realised that there was no point worrying.

Then the next man said: 'Well, we shall never get out of this alive, so we may as well go on with our work while we can.'

57

And that's just what they did. They had every reason to believe that they would be dead soon but, steadily and quietly, they went on digging through the rock face. They went on until the lack of air brought them to their knees exhausted.

Resigned to their fate but pleased they had completed a bit more work at the end, they then lay down and were more astonished than delighted to find themselves rescued in the nick of time. One of the nicest things about this remarkable story is that it gives the lie to the idea that navvies were always and inevitably beyond the pale.

SERMON ON THE TRAIN

ENGLAND, 1846

It is easy to forget how all early railway travel was considered highly dangerous. Not because the trains might crash but more because speed was considered to do untold damage to the human body. There was no evidence to support this view but, at a time when much of science and medicine was still governed by guesswork, it must have seemed merely common sense to propose that since the human body could not, unaided, travel at 20 miles per hour it could not possibly continue to function normally if some means were found to propel it at that reckless speed. Thus, in the first decades of rail travel, children, the infirm, nursing mothers and the elderly would undergo medicals or visit their doctors for advice before considering a train journey.

A writer in the *Quarterly Review* compared the risk of travelling in a railway with that of travelling by rocket. And, in addition to the fear of railway travel, there were moral objections. One bishop insisted that:

> Such things as railway roads and telegraphs are impossible and rank infidelity. There is nothing in the word of God about them, and if God had designed his intelligent creatures to travel at the frightful speed of fifteen miles an hour by steam it would have been foretold by one of His holy prophets. These are the devices of Satan to lead immortal souls to hell.

Late in his long life, the writer and journalist J W Robertson Scott recalled the reactions of a group of his contemporaries to one particular train journey:

Mrs. Carlyle, who was frequently described as a fearless horse-woman, recorded her experience in a train: 'I reached Liverpool after a flight (for it can be called nothing else) of thirty-four miles within an hour and a quarter. I was dreadfully frightened before the train started; it seemed to me certain I should faint; and the impossibility of getting the horrid thing stopt!'

Her husband described the same journey:

The whirl through the confused darkness on those steam wings, one of the strangest things I have experienced – hissing and dashing one knew not whither. Can it be that these terrible Monsters will ever come into general use?

Another passenger said:

On setting off there was a slight jolt arising from the chain catching each carriage, but once in motion we proceeded as smoothly as possible. For a minute or two the pace was gentle. The machine produced little smoke or steam. First in order was the tall chimney, then the boiler – a barrel-like vessel – then an oblong reservoir of water, then a vehicle for coals. The most remarkable moments of the journey were when trains meet. The rapidity is such that there is no recognising the face of a traveller going the other way. The noise on several occasions was like the whizzing of a rocket.

Edith Morley's mother arrived home after her journey and was visited not only by her acquaintances but by many strangers who came to beg for a first-hand account of the experience. She recalled that her baby's bottle had been entrusted to the engine-driver to be kept warm on the engine.

But still the religious objections continued. In 1846 they reached an extraordinary crescendo when a bishop travelled by train moving from carriage to carriage in his full robes and shouting sermons at the other passengers, warning them that further train journeys would certainly lead them to hell and eternal damnation.

PLAYING TRICKS

AMERICA, 1847

In the late 1840s, John S Dunlap was assistant superintendent, or what was then called transportation-master, on the Portland, Oregon line. His brother, George L Dunlap, who eventually became one of the richest men in Chicago, was then a seventeen-year-old clerk in the ticket office. George slept in the big hall over the railway depot on sacking and lived out of a few cardboard boxes. He was famous for playing tricks on passengers, colleagues and even his boss, but he was so well liked that despite this – perhaps even because of this – he was never sacked.

Many of his worst tricks were played on the night watchman, who was nervous at the best of times but particularly so when he made his half-hourly rounds at night. As he went round each time he had to pull a wire leading to a time-clock. Each pull drove a pin in the clock, and if one of these was missing in the morning, it cost him a fine of ten cents.

One dark night, Dunlap lay in wait for the watchman behind a train of freight wagons that had been left in a siding. Dunlap had a box of empty lemonade bottles, and when the poor old watchman came around the corner, peering about to see if anything had gone wrong, Dunlap started throwing the bottles, which fell on the depot platform with such a rattle and a crash that they scared the poor fellow almost out of his senses.

The night watchman grew heartily sick of being teased but there was little he could do until late one night he spotted a shunting engine working alone and lit only by the light of the few fires still

61

burning in the engine shed. He was baffled – no one should be working at this late hour, but he couldn't visit the shed again before completing the rest of his round. He shouted up to Dunlap and told him to go over and check who was working the shunting engine. Dunlap was delighted to be asked to do something – anything – in the middle of the night, since it might give him the chance for a prank or two. He set off across the tracks towards the slowly moving shunting engine while the night watchman headed in the other direction. He'd hardly gone ten paces when he heard an unearthly scream. He turned back and was in time to see Dunlap running as fast as he could away from the shunting engine.

'I saw the controls being worked, I saw them,' Dunlap hissed into the night watchman's face.

'Well, so what if you did?' said the night watchman. 'Who's working that engine, that's what I want to know. He shouldn't be there. Who was it?'

'But that's what I'm trying to tell you,' said the young man. 'The controls are working theirselves. There's no engine driver on the shunter – she's doing it on her own!'

Dunlap took several days off work after that and spent his nights too terrified to sleep. When he returned to work his appetite for pranks had vanished, but it took him some time to realise that he had been the victim of an elaborate hoax. The old night watchman had persuaded a driver friend in the engine shed to work the shunter slowly out of the shed at a given signal and then, as he saw Dunlap approach, he was to jump quietly down from the cab, leaving the shunter moving slowly along on its own.

None of this was made explicit but the young man never played a trick again on the old night watchman.

A MILE A MINUTE

AMERICA, 1848

As late as 1841 it was stated as an astonishing fact by American newspapers that, 'After leaving Boston in the morning, travellers would in fifteen hours be in Albany.' And just ten years later that time had reduced by nearly half. The rate of improvement year by year was astonishing, but by far the most impressive journey of the era in the United States was made in 1848.

Mr Minot, superintendent of the Boston and Maine Railroad in its early days, was a progressive man, always on the alert for improvements that would make his line stand among the first in the country. One day in 1848 he conceived the idea of running a train at the then unheard-of speed of a mile a minute, and once the thought entered his mind he enthusiastically bent every ounce of his energy towards realising it. He had a 10-ton engine built to order at the works of Hinkley and Drury, in Boston, and named it the *Antelope*, in anticipation of its speed.

It had single driving wheels, 6 feet in diameter and Mr Minot watched the progress of the *Antelope* at the works with jealous care, and declared it would either have to run a mile a minute, or go straight back to the factory.

Lawrence, a station 26 miles out of Boston, was chosen by the superintendent as the terminus of the trial trip. Every detail was carefully arranged in order to give the new engine a chance to break all previous records. Nothing escaped the eagle eye of the superintendent. He was especially careful in selecting his men for the run.

'Can you put me in Lawrence in 26 minutes, Pemberton?' he asked of the best engineer on the line.

'It's as good as taking your life in your own hands, sir,' replied Pemberton.

'Not at all,' said Mr Minot, ' If you won't do it, I'll make the run myself.'

As every man on the road knew, the enterprising superintendent, besides being a natural mechanic, and as competent an engineer as ever handled an engine, was unlikely to risk a man's life on a whim.

'Will you do it, Pemberton?' he asked again, as the driver still hesitated.

'Yes, sir.'

'Good – I'll ride with you.'

Once a day had been chosen for the record-breaking speed attempt, platelayers were positioned along the track to make sure every last foot was in perfect order. Stationmasters and signalmen were warned not to permit any obstructions on the track. This was long before telegraphy and Morse code, and to run a mile a minute, a speed until then unheard of, required the utmost planning and forethought as well as careful preparation. All trains were either taken off the rails completely or left in sidings and a slower engine was sent on ahead first to see that all instructions were carried out.

The coming trial of the *Antelope* was talked of far and near, and the event was awaited eagerly in railroad circles. Representatives of the leading Boston papers were invited to accompany the superintendent, and when the appointed day arrived, they, with a few other guests, were given possession of the only carriage that was to be attached to the engine to make the run.

A large crowd gathered at the station and, amid cheers and vast amounts of hat waving, the driver pulled open the throttle, while Mr Minot, who stood by his side, gave a parting salute with his hand.

Slowly the engine gathered speed, then it went thundering on faster and faster, the 6-foot rods annihilating space at a rate previously unheard of. Boston was soon left behind, and the *Antelope* plunged into the open country with the fleetness of the wind, and Mr Minot smiled with pleasure as he kept one eye on the steam-gauge and the other on the rapidly receding fence posts. Everything worked perfectly and the engine seemed to run ever more smoothly the faster it went.

The pace increased still further amid the cheers of the passengers, despite some vicious jolting over rough bits of track, which were numerous in those days, when track laying had not yet been perfected. This only added to the general excitement when the passengers were nearly thrown from their seats as the train plunged around a sharp curve, or narrowly escaped jumping the track. Few of the guests had nerves steady enough to keep them from feeling a little fear for, after all, they were simply taking part in an experiment, and probably travelling faster than any human being had ever travelled before.

On they sped, now past a group of country people whose horses took fright and started off in all directions to escape the snort of the monster. Then the train dashed by a station filled with a wondering crowd whose cheers could be heard for just a split second by the passengers of the lightning express. Mr Minot never lost his confidence in being able to reach Lawrence in 26 minutes because he knew every detail of *Antelope*'s construction.

Halfway to Lawrence, Mr Minot looked at his watch.

'Fourteen minutes!' he shouted to be heard above the rush of wind and steam. 'That won't do, Pemberton; we are a minute behind!'

Shutting his lips more firmly, the driver threw the throttle wide open, and the *Antelope* leapt ever faster along the track. Not a single mishap occurred; all the points were in perfect order, and the rails were checked and tested to the last inch.

At the first glimpse of the town of Lawrence, Mr Minot again looked at his watch. A smile lit up his face and his eyes had a look of exultation. As they neared the station he stood with watch in hand and, just as the engineer brought the train to a standstill, the timepiece marked 26 minutes.

A great crowd awaited the *Antelope*'s arrival, eager to know whether the much-talked-of deed had been accomplished.

'Did you make it?' cried out an excited onlooker.

'We did!' shouted an exultant Mr Minot in return.

In a moment, cheer after cheer arose for the men who had first driven a steam train at the extraordinary speed of a mile a minute.

The guests and the rest of the spectators pressed forward to shake hands with the superintendent and his driver, and to offer congratulations, while crowds flocked from far and near to look at the engine that had accomplished so wonderful a run.

Glowing accounts of the event were given in all the Boston papers, and Mr Minot received an ovation unequalled in the history of the railway.

THUNDERSTORM

AMERICA, 1848

The vast open spaces of America terrified the earliest settlers, who clung for generations to the safer counties of New England and the east. The great unexplored regions of the west were too much for a society that still looked back to the smaller, more densely populated societies from which their ancestors had come in Europe. The Wild West was a vast unknown and was therefore better avoided.

It wasn't until well into the nineteenth century that the railway companies finally began to push out into this unexplored territory. Despite attacks from landowners, and the seemingly insuperable difficulties of the terrain, the railroads gradually moved out into even the most remote corners of the country. But there was a price to pay. Accidents were frequent; railway workers often disappeared into the bush, never to be seen again; supplies and equipment vanished or were stolen. On one or two occasions whole groups of workers were besieged by native tribes for days on end. Occasionally they were massacred and never heard of again. But the most extraordinary disappearing act played out in the Wild West of America had nothing to do with workers, their supplies or equipment. It concerned a whole train.

A huge freight train owned by the Kansas Pacific Company was making its way across country in the 1840s when it got caught in a ferocious thunderstorm. Normally this would have been a relatively minor inconvenience but the storm turned out to be one of the worst of the century and at its heart was a giant waterspout with all the power of a whirlwind.

More than sixteen thousand feet of track were washed away when the eye of the storm passed over a particularly remote part of the railroad. Unfortunately, the train was somewhere on that stretch of track when it happened. Whether it plunged into a canyon with a vast and very deep river at the bottom of it or simply came off the track and was quickly buried in deep sand driven by the extraordinary winds no one knows. But forty years later, after numerous careful searches, the last rather perfunctory attempt to locate the train was carried out. Not a trace of it could be found. To this day its whereabouts remain a mystery.

MY FIRST VISIT TO LONDON

ENGLAND, 1848

John Neeve Masters experienced train travel for the first time when he caught the 9.20am from Headcorn in Kent into London, in the days when railway carriages were still like open cattle trucks. His train was made up of six railway coaches and an engine with a chimney that was so tall it had to be hinged so it could be let down to allow the train to go through tunnels.

The carriages were fitted with hard benches – 'Oh how I longed for a cushion!' recalled Masters – fitted round the sides but there was also a bench running down the centre. The sides of the carriages were high – so high, in fact, that passengers had to stand up to see over them. What astonished Masters initially was the pleasure the other passengers took in continually spitting on the floor of the carriage.

But then they were off. Years later Masters recalled both the dirt and the intense excitement of those first accelerating moments:

Well, off we went and the smoke from the engine nearly smothered us. Most people coughed, but some of us who had never been in a railway train before made out we were enjoying the all-enveloping smog. The terror and thrill of it was certainly something to be remembered. The engine had a longer chimney than locomotives have now and the chimney had to be let down when we passed under a bridge over the railway line, which was pretty often.

Then it came on to rain and most people had got a carriage umbrella, so up went those big umbrellas and down came the drips. I can, in imagination, feel them running down my back even now.

Masters went on to say that his heart was in his mouth for most of the journey, so dangerous and futuristic did the roaring monster seem, but from this most modern method of transport he quickly reverted to something he knew better:

Well, Father and I got to London Bridge station all right – Charing Cross station had yet to be built and we stayed at an ancient inn in Aldersgate Street. We took a horse drawn cab and I can still hear the cabby swearing that Temple Bar – the old arch that was built over the Strand – made life almost impossible because it caused such a bottleneck, but I was sorry when it was pulled down twenty years afterwards.

BATTLE OF THE RAILWAY COMPANIES

ENGLAND, 1849

The Manchester, Sheffield and Lincoln Railway company shared a station in Manchester with the North Western Railway company. At a time when each railway company invariably had its own stations and track this was a cause of endless trouble.

In fact, it got so bad that on numerous occasions when a group of staff from one company bumped into a group of staff from the other company either on the platforms or around the booking hall or goods yard, they would shout abuse at each other or even begin fighting.

Fighting was rare, but individuals from each company would at the very least ignore each other if they happened to meet. Then, late in the 1840s, what had always been a bad situation suddenly became much worse. A Manchester, Sheffield and Lincoln train arrived at platform six early one July morning and the staff of the North Western were ready and waiting: as the passengers climbed down from the train they were arrested and taken to a large waiting room where they were held under lock and key for several hours.

The officials who'd locked the passengers up spent two hours arguing with officials from the Manchester Sheffield and Lincoln company before the police were called and the passengers released. The MSLR sued the North Western company. In court, the MSLR lawyers claimed that the North Western Railway had carried out a continual and flagrant war against the MSLR; they had, it was claimed, deliberately left a truck on a platform designated for use by the MSLR; they had deliberately blocked a line used by the MSLR;

71

they had even, in the dead of night, employed carpenters to build wooden screens across parts of the station used by the MSLR. Worst of all they had bricked up the entrance to the MSLR booking office and then claimed it was an accident!

The judge found for the plaintiff and the NWR were ordered to pay a huge fine. In a case that was and is probably unique in legal history, the whole company, including its directors, was bound over to keep the peace and the company was warned that if they interfered again with the MSLR, their directors might find themselves in prison.

BARKING BABY

ENGLAND, 1849

For the first thirty years of their existence, the railway companies charged very high fares for pets. The feeling was that animals were a bit of a nuisance and might put off other passengers. High prices would ensure that only the absolutely determined would take Rover or Tiddles with them. And if they could afford the high prices, the idea was that pet owners were far more likely to turn up with a spotless poodle rather than a muddy hound, thus reducing the risk of complaints from other passengers.

The high price policy seemed to be having the desired effect, but then rumours began to circulate that passengers were avoiding paying for the pets in the most ingenious ways.

An official who was employed by one company to find out what was going on reported one incident to the board:

> I was aboard the down train for Nottingham, keeping my wits about me, and observing the very mixed crowd in the second class carriages. We stopped at a country station and a woman got into the carriage carrying a ponderous looking babe. It was dressed in long clothes, with its head entirely concealed in a shawl. Several times during the journey the half smothered infant made a noise very like the barking of a dog. The repetition of these unusual sounds aroused the sympathy of another passenger, an old lady, who remarked: 'What a dreadful cold that child has got to be sure.' The woman with the baby replied that the poor thing had suffered

73

an attack of the flu which she was afraid would turn to whooping cough.

At Nottingham, the ticket collector opened the door abruptly and shouted 'Tickets please!' the suddenness of this outburst clearly surprised the slumbering object in the woman's arms and there was an angry and unmistakable bark. The astonished ticket collector reached forward and, before the woman could object, he lifted the shawl to reveal a not particularly attractive nor youthful Dachshund.

The official report does not say what happened next but it is easy to imagine that the poor woman would have had to pay the extra fare amid hoots of laughter from the other passengers.

FUEL GATHERING

ENGLAND, 1850

News that a train was to pass through a rural area spread rapidly; the prospect of the train's arrival was so exciting that people would walk for miles to reach the tracks and they would arrive early and wait all day if necessary to get a good place at the front and so avoid the risk of missing the great event.

A journalist waiting with a huge crowd to see a train pass in the South-West was astonished to see – when the train finally arrived – that the tender seemed to have all sorts of rubbish in it in addition to the coal. There were bits of old wooden furniture, fencing, even whole small trees. He made some enquiries but came up against a wall of silence and denial. Coal was the only fuel ever used, he was told.

The journalist was convinced by what he'd seen so he began to travel regularly along the line. On his first few trips nothing untoward happened but then, for no apparent reason, the train stopped in the middle of nowhere and, on looking out the window, the journalist saw the driver and the fireman leap down from the engine and run into a wood nearby. They came back with armfuls of logs, loaded them on to the train and then ran back to an old, apparently abandoned farmhouse and proceeded to help themselves to the logs piled up in the garden. They also ripped out the side of a wooden chicken house and tore up the wooden palings that ran along the drive to the house. It took them nearly an hour to load up the tender again with the various bits and pieces they'd stolen and they did it amid howls of protest

75

from the passengers, who shouted from the windows of the train that the delay would make them late for various appointments.

When the journalist later wrote his report the editor spiked it – he was also a shareholder in the local railway!

THE SOOT BAG MEN

ENGLAND, 1850

The early railway prided itself on the fact that its first-class service attracted the well-to-do, the successful and the more adventurous of the aristocracy. Refinements to the service were always aimed at first-class passengers and at the groups who could be assumed to enjoy travelling in some style. After all, this is where the greatest profits were to be made. And it is easy to imagine the railway owners lamenting the fact that it was necessary, merely to keep the wheels of commerce in motion, also to provide third-class coaches, or wagons, as they might better be described.

Third class made little in the way of profit for the railway company owners but factory owners who might have a share or two in railway stock wanted cheap transport for their staff. Imagine, then, the horror of the railway directors when they heard rumours that the well-to-do were, in increasing numbers, buying third-class tickets.

One director simply could not believe that this was happening so he spent several weeks travelling each day on one of the early up trains to London. He discovered that a significant proportion of those who, judging by their dress, should have known better, were happily asleep or reading their newspapers in carriages made to carry only those lesser mortals who dug the roads, or cleaned the sewers. Those behaving badly included landowners, gentleman farmers and even, God help us, the odd baronet.

In short, first class had invaded third, an event that hinted at the worst kind of revolutionary fervour and, worse still, meant a loss of funds for the railway directors and shareholders. This situation could not be allowed to continue. But a solution was hard to find – booking office clerks could hardly be asked to refuse to issue third-class tickets to anyone who seemed able to afford first class.

The director reported the situation to his fellow directors:

I discovered that there were certain persons in superior positions who were base enough to travel third class and in order to bring these offenders to a proper sense of their position and to swell the revenues of the company, I recommend that we introduce what might best be termed special inconveniences.

The lead was taken in this respect by the Manchester and Leeds Railway, the directorate of which brought in what was known as the 'soot bag system'.

Thus on a bright spring morning in 1850 one of the most extraordinary journeys in railway history began. A team of four chimney sweeps had been specially hired. Each was assigned a third-class carriage that was believed to harbour individuals who did not belong to the working classes.

The decision about which carriages needed 'special inconveniences' was based on observations made by a senior porter who watched to see if anyone well turned out entered a third-class carriage. He then kept a note and reported his findings to the sweeps.

As soon as the train set off on its journey the sweeps moved into action. They entered the third-class carriages and immediately unfolded several of their recently used sacks and began to shake them out, thus covering everyone in the carriage with a layer of grime and dirt. The working men, of course, took little or no notice, since their work obliged them to wear rough and dirty clothes anyway. But the well dressed were outraged. What could they do, though? If they complained to the management they would be told to travel first class, since third-class passengers were used to dust and dirt and the railway company could do nothing about it.

The ruse worked and the numbers of passengers travelling first class rose and as time passed fewer of the middle classes risked a confrontation with the soot bag men.

According to an early edition of *The Railway Times*, other rail companies found it more convenient to make sure that sheep or even pigs travelled regularly in their third-class carriages!

HIGH-SPEED JUDGES

ENGLAND, 1850

The four elderly judges, sent up as a special commission to try some rioters at Stafford, went by special train from Euston. According to *The Railway Times*, none had ever travelled by rail before and they were at best apprehensive, at worst terrified. All had said special goodbyes to their families and had checked their wills and that their affairs were in order before setting out.

Lord Abinger, presiding in the Court of Exchequer, on hearing that the judges had travelled by rail, said they were foolish in the extreme to allow themselves to be propelled through the air at a speed for which God had not designed the human body. Even if he were called as a witness, he insisted, and compelled to attend the court, he would refuse to travel by rail whatever the risk of prosecution for contempt of court.

In the event, the judges survived the journey but found the experience of travelling at speeds in excess of 30 miles per hour so exhilarating that they could think of nothing else for weeks afterwards. Such were their high spirits that the rioters were let off with far more lenient sentences than would otherwise have been the case.

SMOKING SIGNS

ENGLAND, 1851

It is difficult now to believe it, but in Victorian times male travellers didn't like travelling with the fairer sex. This had a great deal to do with the fact that relations between the sexes were far more formal then than now. One book of travel etiquette published in the 1840s recommends that gentlemen entering a carriage where a lady is already seated should first bow to her and then ask permission to take a seat in the same compartment. The book goes on to explain that under no circumstances should a gentleman take snuff or smoke in the presence of a lady. Newspaper reading was, however, acceptable, although novels might cause offence if they were in French, since anything French was considered to be, almost by definition, notoriously scandalous.

The situation became so bad on some routes out of London that an enterprising printer began a profitable sideline selling smoking signs. These were advertised discreetly through gentlemen's clubs and sold to men who had in the past had to endure a journey with a female. The signs were hugely popular, but once you had your sign it was still essential to arrive at the station in time to get a compartment alone or with a fellow male. Once in a compartment with no women, the trick was to stick one of the carefully faked – but authentic looking – smoking signs on the window facing the platform and on the window facing the corridor.

If the rules for men were onerous they were even worse for female travellers. A woman on her own would not enter a compartment where a single man was seated, although it was acceptable if he was accompanied by his wife or a child. However, no single woman with any pretensions to good breeding would dream of entering a smoking compartment with one or more males.

It was only when railway staff began to notice that on some journeys virtually every compartment was designated a smoking compartment that officials realised something was amiss. More careful records were kept and ticket collectors were instructed to check the actual number of smoking compartments compared with the official list. No one was ever arrested for the scam – the ticket collectors were simply instructed discreetly to remove illegal signs. Among the smoking classes this was seen as a black day indeed.

SEEING THE DEVIL

ENGLAND, 1851

It is difficult today to appreciate quite how terrifying the first sight of a locomotive engine must have been, particularly for people in remote rural districts who had nothing in their own past lives to help them comprehend this extraordinary apparition. In the early nineteenth century the world was governed entirely by the pace set by the horse and the idea that a mechanical contraption with no horse could travel at twice the speed of the fastest horse, and for hours on end, must have seemed not just fanciful but downright impossible. There are numerous accounts in diaries of country people who, after reading about the coming of the railway in their newspapers, regarded the idea as a joke made up by journalists to fool the more credulous. There are also accounts of people seeing their first train and simply fainting or running away. A vicar took his eight-year-old son to see the very first train pass through Devon and the boy screamed and ran away and apparently had nightmares for weeks afterwards.

Perhaps the most amusing story of shock at the arrival of the iron railroad comes from a Midlands writer who recorded the words of an old lady from a village in the hills who came down to visit some relatives in a town on the newly opened North Midland Railway. On her first day wandering about the town she saw her first train.

Rushing into her relatives' house, almost beside herself with panic, she screamed:

Oh Bessie! What dusta think awve sane? Awve sane t'divil his-self. 'is yed wor all ablaze and smokin and he rushed along over faelds and 'edges and jumpin ditches and then ey sqealed loike a pig oinly 'arder. I nivir want to see im no more!

SABBATH TRAINS

SCOTLAND, 1851

The first trains to run through Scotland in the middle decades of the nineteenth century caused outrage among the more religious inhabitants who, in some cases, knelt by the side of the tracks to pray for deliverance from the fire-breathing monster sent by the devil to corrupt the Sabbath.

An Englishman arriving at Edinburgh station in the 1850s was collared by a Presbyterian as he alighted on the platform. With gimlet eye, the zealot harangued the poor traveller with the following words:

> And if we are entitled to employ our servants for railway work on the Sabbath why am not I and others entitled to reap our crops, or plough our fields on that day, or why may not a manufacturer also employ his work-people or any other work whatever be carried on? Is there any exemption for railway work or have they any privilege above any other system of labour? If once Sabbath work on the railway commences, the system will rapidly spread to every other occupation and then we are doomed, doomed...

The traveller disengaged himself and vowed to keep his Scottish travels to the minimum.

TRAIN UNDER ARREST

ENGLAND, 1852

On its own land, a railway company is a very powerful organisation, which is why railway police exist. Trespassers on railway property, passengers travelling without a ticket, individuals interfering with railway property – all are liable to be arrested and dealt with severely by the courts. For the railway was and is an important institution. But the most extraordinary arrest ever made in conjunction with the railway occurred in 1852.

It stemmed from a disagreement between the Great Northern Railway and the Midland Railway. The Great Northern claimed the right to run its own engines and trains into the Midland station at Nottingham. But the claim, and the right it bestowed, had never been tested and few thought it ever would be. That is, until the Great Northern decided it would act on the basis of its claimed rights.

On 1 August it attempted to run one of its trains into the station, but the Midland Railway company was prepared and the trespassing train – if indeed it was trespassing – was arrested. Midland engines appeared as if from nowhere, as the Great Northern train approached the station. One got behind the interloper, the other in front. The Great Northern train was effectively boxed in and had to do as it was told. The Great Northern driver made a gallant attempt to power his way out of the situation, despite the two foreign locomotives. But one engine is never a match for two and the train was carried off to a Midland engine shed once the passengers had been allowed to get off. And there in the shed it was left under lock and key. Just to be sure there was absolutely no chance of rescue, the rails leading to the shed were then pulled up and there the train remained a prisoner until peace was concluded between the two railway companies almost a year later.

WIDOW TO THE RESCUE

AMERICA, 1854

The Western Division of the Virginia Railroad Company ran through a very mountainous part of the state and stations were few and far between. About three miles from one of these stations the track ran through a deep gorge of the Blue Ridge. At the centre of the gorge – a place about as remote as it possible could be – there was a tiny cabin surrounded by a few acres of fruit trees. The cabin was inhabited by a widow called Graff and her three young daughters.

In the summer, the three daughters walked together each day to the nearest station carrying baskets of berries, which they sold to passengers weary of packed lunches and stale beer and tea. The money they earned was a useful supplement to a pitifully small farm income and their mother's Civil War widow's pension.

The regular conductor on the once-a-day train knew the girls well and when they'd sold their fruit at the station he often invited them to jump aboard and then signalled the driver to make an unauthorised stop where the track passed the children's farmstead. The children always offered to pay the conductor for his kindness by giving him any remaining baskets of fruit. He would always accept but insisted on paying.

Then came the worst winter in living memory. The year 1854 saw snow more than three feet deep right across the state and in some places, where drifts had built up, it was twenty or thirty feet deep. Then, in mid-December of that year, the weather suddenly turned warm, causing the snow to melt rapidly. This was combined with a series of terrible storms, so that the valleys were filled with raging water, from hill tops swept by ferocious winds.

On 26 December the Western Division train was making its way through the Blue Ridge with its friendly conductor aboard. Despite the pitch black, the howling wind and the torrential rain the guard was not worried because the track had been built along a bed of solid rock and it was impossible that somewhere up ahead it might have been swept away. As he walked through his train the guard tried to reassure the obviously worried passengers that they were in no danger, despite the fact that the train was visibly rocking under the onslaught of the elements.

Then, just before midnight, there was a piercing shriek from the driver's whistle. The conductor and his guards applied the brakes immediately and the train quickly came to a halt. When the conductor ran to the front of the train and stood by the driver an extraordinary sight met his eyes. Out in front of the train, for twenty or thirty feet and more, a huge pile of logs was blazing. What on earth was going on? Driver and conductor jumped down and walked the length of the fire. Beyond it, just a hundred feet or so, the track vanished into an abyss.

The combination of huge snow drifts followed by torrential rain and flooding had torn the whole side of the mountain out. The widow Graff and her daughters had seen the huge slide of earth and rock and realised what would happen if they did not act. They knew the train was due in a few hours so they spent that time going back and forth to their stockpile of brushwood and logs, building the fire that had saved the train and its occupants from certain destruction.

Despite the tempest, all the passengers climbed down to see the huge fire that had saved their lives. They were so grateful that they made a collection for the widow that amounted to nearly $500 – a large sum in the mid-nineteenth century. At first the widow wouldn't take the money but she was eventually persuaded and she used it to send her daughters to school – something that would have been impossible otherwise.

The railway company was so grateful that they built the widow and her daughters a new house and gave the whole family lifetime free passes to travel whenever and wherever they liked on the railroad.

LOST IN THE SNOW

AMERICA, 1855

In the days of old, when whole trains would scarcely weigh as much as one engine does now, a big snowstorm was the greatest dread of railroad men in the United States. A bad snowstorm would almost certainly mean being stuck in the country, miles away from any house, for two or three days at least. In many cases it was much worse and trains might be stuck for a week or more.

The winter of 1855 was worse than any in living memory. Huge swathes of the country vanished under a deep blanket of snow and the blizzards seemed unending. At Aurora, Illinois, a certain well-known character, Colonel W S Johnson, narrowly escaped death from hypothermia, after getting stuck on a train journey in huge drifts. Six men lost their lives in that particular storm, within a few miles of the spot where Colonel Johnson had such a narrow escape.

For sixteen days, trains without number were buried under the mountains of snow that blanketed the prairie. It then took weeks to dig them all out, but, when the thaw came, two further freight trains that had been entirely forgotten simply appeared as if from nowhere as the snows began to melt. The railroad companies had been thrown into such turmoil by the loss of so many trains and by the general chaos that they'd managed to forget two whole trains!

THE REAL GREAT TRAIN ROBBERY

ENGLAND, 1855

When people think of the Great Train Robbery they think of the crude, bungled two million-pound heist in 1963. But that robbery was nothing compared to the Great Train Robbery of 1855. When the mastermind behind the 1855 crime was eventually caught – and his capture had nothing to do with any failure in the execution of the robbery – even the judge described the man behind the theft as a genius.

That genius was Edward Agar, a man about whom little was known before he became famous for his extraordinary exploits on the London to Folkestone train.

By his own admission a career criminal, Agar had amassed a small fortune before deciding to risk all on his most daring crime. Although he was in his forties at the time of the crime he had never once before been caught for any offence.

Agar knew a corrupt lawyer called Barrister Saward who, in turn, was friendly with a fellow gambler called Pierce. Pierce had been sacked from the South Eastern Railway for his addiction to gambling and Saward had turned to crime to pay off his own huge gambling debts. The two men knew each other well, so when Pierce heard from his former railway colleagues that huge loads of gold bullion were regularly carried from London to Folkestone by train (from whence they were ferried across the English Channel and then on to Paris) he suggested to his friend, Saward, that they steal one of the shipments. Saward turned to Agar, the greatest safe breaker of the age, to see if it could be done.

Through meticulous study and preparation Agar had built a flawless criminal career. The same attention to detail enabled him to make some startling discoveries about the gold shipments. They were always carried in 3 foot-square solid steel safes made by Chubb, whose new locks were said to be unpickable. Each safe had two keys. One was held by the stationmaster at London Bridge, from where the trains departed. The other was held by the stationmaster at Folkestone. Inside the inch-thick steel of the safes the gold was stored in locked bullion chests, which also carried the bank's seals. These were checked before departure, again at Folkestone and finally at their destination in Paris, where two further keys were held. Agar concluded that the robbery was totally impossible and told Saward so. That seemed to be the end of the matter but then fortune intervened to change everything.

Agar's mistress was friendly with a guard on the South Eastern, one James Burgess, who was disgruntled at the fact that railwaymen's wages had declined as the railway boom ended. He quickly became one of the conspirators, as did William Tester, the superintendent's assistant at London Bridge. The accident of fortune that made the robbery possible was the loss – by the company – of one of their two keys to the train safe. The railway company directors were so worried about this that they sent the safe back to Chubb's and new locks and keys were fitted. The correspondence over the work came through the hands of Tester, who slipped out of the office with the keys on the day they were returned from Chubb's and met Agar in a nearby pub. He was back with the keys within ten minutes but that was long enough for Agar to have taken an impression of the keys in a tin of wax.

Unfortunately, in his haste, Tester had brought two copies of the same key. The other was still beyond the conspirators' reach. It was the Folkestone key they still needed. To get it, Agar went to Folkestone one evening and walked along the pier to the little office where the key was kept. When the office closed he smoked the lock using a narrow, hollow metal cylinder that had been split lengthways in two and blackened with candle smoke. The technique of smoking was to slide the two halves of the cylinder into the lock until they covered the central spindle of the mechanism; once inserted the two halves of the narrow steel cylinder were turned and then carefully removed. They would then carry in the blackened smoke areas of metal the clear markings of the levers. Using this, Agar made a key that would open the lock. Agar then sent himself a box of gold sovereigns to be collected at the office on the pier. The gold was carried, as Agar knew it would be, on the mail train and in Chubb's safe. When he went to collect his gold, the stationmaster, seeing a highly respectable figure standing before him, didn't worry for a second when he unlocked a small cabinet on the wall, took out the Chubb safe key and set off for the train to collect Agar's gold.

In the ten minutes he was out Agar was able to make a wax impression of the little cabinet's key. He then collected his gold and left. That night he was back. He entered the office, opened the cabinet and took an impression of the second Chubb key. He now had both keys to the impregnable Chubb railway safe. To make sure the copies would work, Agar sneaked aboard the London Bridge Folkestone mail train when no gold was being shipped. Burgess let him into the guard's van, where he tried the keys and then filed them until they were perfect.

On 15 May the robbery began. Pierce climbed aboard the mail train at London Bridge carrying two carpet bags, each containing one hundredweight of lead shot. The bags were taken to the guard's van where the Chubb safe was kept. Agar deliberately waited till he'd almost missed the train then leapt aboard the guard's van, just as any late passenger might, as Burgess waved his flag for the off.

London Bridge to Redhill, the train's first stop, gave Agar just over half an hour. He had the two keys and immediately opened the safe. He then used specially prepared pincers and thin levers to ease up the rivets on the steel bands on the bullion chests. With the bands loosened a fraction he was able to drive wedges between the lid of the chest and the base until the lock burst in such a way that the seal was left intact. This meant that on casual inspection at Folkestone all would seem well.

Before the first stop, Agar had removed the gold from one chest and weighed out exactly the same amount of lead shot. This then went back into the bullion chest. The rivets were knocked back into place, the bullion chest replaced in the safe and the safe locked with the keys. At Redhill, Tester was waiting for the bag that was discreetly passed to him from the guard's van. It contained nearly 40 pounds in weight of solid gold bullion. Meanwhile Pierce, who'd been travelling first class, got off the train, walked along the platform and jumped into the guard's van.

As the train headed for Tonbridge, its next stop, Agar emptied the second bullion chest, this time of gold coins. Just as before, the same weight of lead shot was put back in the chest and the chest sealed and replaced in the safe. The same was repeated for the third chest. By the time they reached Tonbridge the two men had more than two hundredweight of gold in bags strapped to their chests and in the two carpet bags that had formerly contained lead shot.

Just before 11pm the train reached Folkestone. The men left the guard's van and walked along the platform before re-boarding the train. At Dover they went back to the guard's van and collected their carpet bags. They stayed for a while in a hotel and then caught the next train back to London. Within a few hours some of the gold had already been turned into untraceable money and still the robbery had not been discovered. The chests passed examination at Folkestone and Boulogne. It was only the following afternoon when the chests were opened in Paris that the theft was discovered. The banks immediately sued the South Eastern Railway. The railway refused to pay up, saying the robbery must have been carried out in France. The French railway service denied everything. Both said the robbery was impossible.

Meanwhile, Agar and Pierce melted the gold down in a house in Kilburn It was quickly disposed of through the crooked barrister Saward.

Agar was only caught more than a year later after he was arrested on an entirely different matter – he was framed by a criminal friend after falling for the man's girlfriend. The crime was forgery and Agar's enemies gave evidence against him. Agar knew he would be transported to Australia for at least twenty years, so he wrote to Pierce asking that he use some of the money from the train robbery to look after his ex-girlfriend and their child. But Pierce cheated both girlfriend and child and, when Agar found out, he decided to give Queen's evidence against his former colleagues and reveal all about the robbery that had baffled the British and French police for more than a year. Pierce was sentenced to two years' hard labour, Tester and Burgess to fourteen years' transportation. Agar's life sentence for forgery stood but, because he had not been found guilty of the train robbery, neither his wealth nor that of his associates could be taken from him and so all of it – millions of pounds in today's money – went to Agar's girlfriend and his child. And with that, Agar, perhaps the greatest of all British criminals, disappears into the annals of history.

SOMETHING TO COMPLAIN ABOUT

ENGLAND, 1856

The tradition of grumbling about the quality of the railway service is as old as the railway service itself. In many cases, some would say most, any amount of grumbling is justified given that the standards the railway owners aspire to are rarely met in practice. But one or two individuals in every generation have taken grumbling to absurd lengths. Indeed, grumbling about train journeys has, for one or two poor souls, virtually become the sole purpose of life. Take, for example, the elderly woman who every day for years berated the poor guard on the 8.50 from London to Cambridge. Despite his patience and professionalism her constant complaints eventually got the better of him. She had treated him to ten minutes of solid invective during which she attacked just about every employee of the railway, its directors and shareholders. More to relieve his frustration than anything he eventually said: 'I will make sure I pass your comments on when I take the chair at the next directors' meeting.'

But a season ticket holder at Chesham in Buckinghamshire in 1856 probably holds the record for grumpiest rail traveller, for this was the year in which he began to travel each day armed with hundreds of brochures and cartoons. He had complained by letter about the railway to local and national newspapers and, despite the fact that some of his letters had been published, he was still not happy – presumably because he did not perceive any improvement in the service, despite his most strenuous efforts. He therefore went to a printer with a mass of vituperative cartoons, skits and libellous satires on the railway company with which he travelled. Having paid to have five thousand copies printed of each cartoon and skit he took bundles of them with him each time he travelled. The idea, one supposes, was to shame the company into new methods of conduct, but whatever his hopes his actions were unambiguous. He took a seat at the front of the train each day and, as the engine slowed at each station, he would throw out liberal handfuls of his publicity material to the waiting passengers.

A typical cartoon showed the company's train being beaten in a race by a donkey and cart; others showed the directors as slumbering dolts. No doubt the directors could have banned their belligerent passenger from travelling on any of their trains. They might even have been able successfully to sue him, but, to their credit, they put up with his campaigns for many months and it was only the danger to other passengers that compelled them finally to act.

It seems that the irate passenger had very real talent as a cartoonist and satirist, which meant that passengers began eagerly to look forward to the shower of paper that came flying out of the windows of the early morning train. In fact, they enjoyed them so much that there was a scramble each morning that could have led to someone being pushed under a train. It was pointed out to the angry traveller that his paper showers might lead to the injury or death of another passenger and that this, in turn, might lead to a prosecution for manslaughter. After that the complaints continued but the paper satires ceased to flutter above the early morning platform.

DOGS ON BOARD

ENGLAND, 1857

The eccentric Earl of Bridgwater never married. He rarely left his estate and, as he grew older, he became ever more slovenly and bizarre in his habits. He made a servant follow him constantly, carrying a large box of snuff; he insisted on wearing a different pair of shoes for every day of the year and he never threw anything away. As a result, his large London house groaned under the weight of old boxes and trunks, umbrellas, chests filled with old curtains, suits and rugs, discarded wrapping papers, broken-down chairs and piles of assorted domestic refuse.

But among all his eccentricities there was one that distinguished Bridgwater from every other eccentric aristocrat in the land: his love for his dogs. He owned about fifteen and he treated them as if they were his children. Some were strays he'd taken a fancy to while walking the streets; others were pure-bred hounds and gundogs, still others were tiny lapdogs. All were allowed to sleep with the earl and to eat with him.

Indeed, every day the earl would have his huge dining room laid with the best linen and silver cutlery and each of the dogs would sit in a chair in its allotted place. The dogs were expected to dress for dinner and the only time the earl shouted at the dogs was if they happened to misbehave during the meal.

Several times a year the earl travelled by train from London to his home in the country. Normally one or two dogs would accompany him, but on one extraordinary occasion all fifteen dogs set out for the London terminus. The earl paid for fifteen first-class tickets for the dogs and took over two whole compartments. To make sure no stranger tried to enter one of the two compartments – this was in the days when compartments could not be reserved – he sent his servants on ahead to the station to bar the entrances to the carriages in advance of the earl and his party of dogs arriving at the station.

During the journey each dog took a seat in one or other of the compartments and the earl wandered between the two making sure his favourites were enjoying themselves. Other passengers looking for a vacant seat found the blinds of the compartments drawn and the earl's own reserved signs posted on the windows.

On this never-to-be-forgotten journey, the earl fell asleep and, on waking, went to check on the dogs. He found to his horror that six dogs – 'I'd never met them before,' he declared later – had somehow joined his favourites. Unused to strange dogs, the earl's normally well-behaved hounds had gone almost berserk – they were barking and jumping and even biting each other.

It took the earl and his servants some time to restore order and to reject the interlopers. He was so outraged by what he described as a serious violation that he threatened the railway company with legal action and it was only a personal visit from one of the directors that smoothed the troubled waters. Though the railway company officials privately agreed that the earl was a damned nuisance he was a good customer with powerful friends – so the doggy train journeys continued, but so far as history records attest, without further mishap.

DUNG ROAMIN'

SCOTLAND, 1860

Mr Lubbock, an amateur engineer from Dudley in the West Midlands, was travelling on the North of Scotland Railway. The train had stopped at a station but, despite a great deal of huffing and puffing, the engine, having stopped, refused to get started again.

Mr Lubbock was irritated as he had an appointment two stops further on and hated being late. He went up to the engine and spoke to the driver and the fireman. They explained that they couldn't move because certain tubes in the engine were leaking, but help – they insisted – would be with them soon. Mr Lubbock assumed this meant the arrival by some other means of a spare part or two, so he was astonished to see a farmer approaching across the fields with a bucket, which turned out to be filled with horse manure.

There was a practice – described as almost universal in the early days of steam – of putting oatmeal or bran or, if these could not be found, horse dung into the boiler in order to stop the leaking of the tubes.

Mr Lubbock watched as the horse dung disappeared into the boiler and then got back into his compartment. Within minutes the train pulled out of the station as if nothing was amiss.

THE MAN WHO WASN'T THERE

ENGLAND, 1860

Victorian carriages were dark, dingy and sometimes forbidding. Lit only by oil lamps they permitted an occasional robbery of a sleeping passenger and on at least one occasion the dim glow of oil allowed a night train passenger to vanish. It was always assumed he was murdered but no body was ever found. He'd been travelling on a train lit by oil lamps enclosed in heavy glass containers, about nine inches in diameter, hung through holes in the carriage roofs. These lamps were dropped into their places by a man who got on to the roof by climbing the steps at the end of the carriages. The glass lamps, wheeled along the platform in a bogey truck, which had frames for them to rest in, were thrown up to the man on the carriage roofs, who caught them with a bit of cotton waste in one hand in order to prevent their slipping. After him came a man who walked along the roofs to light the lamps.

The lamps are relevant to the mystery of the man who disappeared, as we will see. This man began his journey innocently enough, although it was later said that he was carrying a suitcase that had been chained to his wrist. When the train entered a long tunnel on the Brighton line, our mysterious passenger was asleep; when it came out the other end of the tunnel he had gone. His friends waiting at the station were mystified by his non-arrival. Passers-by later reported that these so-called friends had been a shabby, strange and foreign-looking bunch who dispersed without a word after it became clear that the man for whom they had waited was not going to appear.

But whatever the truth about these suspicious characters was, it is certainly true that they did not go aboard the train and check each carriage, nor did they report the disappearance of their friend to the police. Instead they melted into the night and were never heard of again. Meanwhile, routine cleaning of the carriages discovered the mysterious passenger's hat and leather overnight bag as well as his ticket. There were also traces of a sticky tar-like substance on the open window of the carriage and one of the overhead oil lamps had been dislodged and smashed. Below it a light dusting of white powder, later found to contain traces of arsenic, had settled on the carriage seat and floor. But there were no footprints in the dust.

The London terminus where the oil lamps had been tended at the beginning of the journey employed a number of railwaymen to do the work. On the day following the disappearance of the passenger, one of these workers also vanished. What happened to 'the man who wasn't there', and indeed to the lamp man, remains a mystery to this day.

MAD WINDHAM

ENGLAND, 1861

Anyone travelling on the Eastern Counties Railway in the early1860s might have been surprised to come across a railwayman with a difference. For on different days this absurdly well-spoken railwayman with an aristocratic demeanour and rather haughty air would appear as a porter, a driver or a fireman. What was even more remarkable about him was that he worked for no pay. The railwayman in question was William Frederick Windham, or Mad Windham as he became known.

Windham was born in 1840, the heir to ancient Felbrigg Hall in Norfolk and all its estates. He was worth a fortune but by the end of his short life he'd squandered or given all of it away. He once said that the only time he was truly happy was when he was on the footplate of a locomotive engine, which is why he tried every means in his power to get on to the trains that plied their trade across East Anglia.

The extent of his railway work came to light when, soon after inheriting his estates, Windham was taken to court by his family. The family wanted him declared insane for marrying a prostitute, for rushing about the country throwing money away and for impersonating a railwayman. What they really wanted was for the court to agree that anyone rich enough not to have to work on the railway must be mad to want to do it.

According to the evidence given at Windham's trial, his manners and conduct were uncouth, his mental powers well below the average and his wilfulness both extreme and bizarre.

103

Certainly Windham had hated his upbringing, with its emphasis on the traditional sports and pastimes of the aristocracy. Hunting and shooting held no interest for him and all his talk was of railways. But kept from the things he really wanted to do, Windham grew ever more eccentric. Wherever he happened to be, and however embarrassing the circumstances, he might suddenly shout with unmeaning laughter, or imitate cats fighting, or burst into tears, or get pitifully drunk. 'Take away this disagreeable boy,' the indignant mothers of young girls would exclaim when he was taken, as a child, to other people's houses.

By preference, he sought his amusements elsewhere. As he grew towards manhood, his tutors found it difficult to restrain him from doing pretty much as he wished; and the last of them, a Mr Peatfield, who was appointed in June 1860, seems to have had little control over him at any time. This was about the time Windham began to bribe and cajole engine drivers into letting him drive their trains, an accomplishment of which he was extremely proud. But he was equally happy when acting as guard, ticket collector, sorter of parcels, or porter. He obtained a guard's uniform, with belt, pouch and whistle; and in this guise he became a familiar figure on the Eastern Counties Railway. Railway officials indulged his whims to an almost incredible extent. On one occasion – unquestionably the railway journey he enjoyed most – he was driver in the morning, guard in the afternoon and porter in the evening. It was 1861. This remarkable day was only marred when, by blowing his whistle at the wrong moment, he nearly caused a serious accident on the Suffolk line.

When in London, he used to haunt the Haymarket, at that time the centre of the city's night life. He frequented London's brothels and was much in the company of prostitutes but, on the whole, he seems to have found greater enjoyment in pretending to be a policeman in town and a railwayman while in the country. Although they did not provide him with a uniform, the police showed him the same kindly indulgence as the railway officials had done. They looked on tolerantly when he went up to groups of people in the street and ordered them, in the voice and manner of a policeman, to move on.

He used to threaten women that he would have them locked up –
he said there were too many women in the Haymarket, and that he
would not stand it any longer. The women would shout back, 'Go
away, you fool; you're not right in your head!'

By the time he'd come into his inheritance, he'd met and married
Agnes Willoughby, allegedly a prostitute. She was said to belong to
the same circle as famous mistresses of the aristocracy and royalty,
women such as Catherine Walters – alias Skittles – who appears in
many Victorian memoirs.

Once they were married, Agnes managed to persuade Windham
to sign all his money and property over to her. But, despite this and
his passion for the railways, the courts refused to declare him
insane. The biggest problem was that Windham seemed to the
courts no madder than many family members brought to testify
against him. But once the court had made its decision and he was
released Windham headed for the brothels of London and the
railways of East Anglia with a vengeance. Having been thrown out
of Felbrigg Hall by Agnes he rented a room in a coaching inn in
Norwich where he spent his days permanently dressed as a railway
guard and staring out of his bedroom window, from which position
he would shout and make faces at the ostlers. At last in February
1866 he died after a massive bout of drinking and still in his railway
guard's uniform.

IMPERSONATING A COW

FRANCE, 1862

Excursion trains were by no means an exclusively English phenomenon. The French took to the idea with a passion in the 1860s – so much so that on the Paris-Le Havre line they often ran short of proper carriages. In any other country the railway company would have bought extra carriages, or borrowed some from another train company. Not the French. Without worrying about how the excursion passengers would feel about it, they simply added open cattle trucks to any over-booked excursion train. These were fitted with the crudest of seats in the form of rough planks laid across wooden blocks.

On one cattle truck excursion the passengers at first accepted the situation with good humour, but when a ticket inspector entered one of the trucks to check that everyone had paid, some strange collective lunacy took hold of the passengers and they answered every question posed by the official with a loud collective 'Moo!'

The joke did not end there either, for soon it had extended to all the other cattle trucks and, unable to get anything other than animal noises out of any of the passengers, the inspector could do nothing but beat a hasty retreat.

At the next station the stationmaster tried to restore some order and dignity to the proceedings by donning his very best top hat and addressing the train from the top of an apple box. After two sentences his words were drowned out by a chorus of moos.

According to the reports that appeared the next day in a local newspaper the situation grew even worse when the train reached its destination. The passengers in the cattle trucks rushed the barrier en masse, knocking inspectors, porters and other staff out of their way.

When the stationmaster managed to grab one of the passengers, the others turned on him and – still pretending to be cows – ran at him with their heads down. After he'd been butted in the stomach by the sixth or seventh cow-imitating passenger he released the man he'd grabbed and ran for the safety of his ticket office. At that point, and for reasons which have never been explained, the crowd as one suddenly stopped their bovine antics, quietly handed over their tickets and filed out of the station.

DARING FEAT

AMERICA, 1862

The train consisted of a luggage van or baggage car and two passenger coaches, with the engine *General Stark*, which had just been delivered from the Massachusetts-based Lawrence Locomotive Works. The driver was Dick Allen, who later achieved fame as Richard Norton Allen, the wealthy Cleveland inventor and businessman.

About five miles from Bennington, Vermont, the train hit a cow and the engine and two carriages were thrown off the track. Driver and conductor were uninjured so they picked themselves up, sat on the track and discussed what they should do. The only way to get another engine was to run a hand-car – one of those absurd little rail carts with a rocking handle you see in Westerns – or walk. Neither prospect appealed, so they thought again.

'It's nearly all downhill to Bennington,' said the driver. 'So let's uncouple the last carriage and run it back on its own to the station.'

Today, anything like this would lead to an inquiry and the instigators would almost certainly be sacked. But in the early days – particularly in America, with its huge distances between towns – quick expedients and great risks were often necessary.

After the passengers had been persuaded to get out of the last carriage, the guard, a brakeman and the conductor uncoupled it. With a gentle push it began to pick up speed on the steep incline. The three men leapt aboard as it began to move.

At first everything went smoothly and the conductor later described the strange sensation of speed with no noise – or at least no noise other than the whistling of the wind. But the three men were anything but relaxed – what on earth would they do, they wondered, if they should reach an uphill stretch of track?

As it turned out, Fortune was with them, and the momentum they'd gained took them over each and every rising stretch of track and on to yet another downhill section. The one exception – a stretch too steep and in danger of stopping them dead – was overcome when two of the three men jumped down and added their pushing power to the carriage's impetus. The effort proved effective and the carriage inched over the top of the rise to begin its descent once again. A wandering cow posed the next threat, but with shouts and gesticulations they managed to frighten it off the track ahead, and, soon afterwards, the carriage rolled into the station with the brakeman furiously turning his handle to slow it down.

With a relief engine they started back to the scene of the accident, pulled the other engine back on to the track and went on to Rutland at terrific speed. The *General Stark*, despite coming off the rails, was undamaged, and they made it to their destination only an hour or so late. It was a train rescue long remembered and talked about in the annals of American railway history.

PULLING THE CORD

ENGLAND, 1862

The emergency services are plagued with trivial telephone calls. The elderly will, we are told, regularly call for an ambulance if they find it too difficult to carry their shopping up the stairs; young women have been known to telephone for help if a long and delicately painted fingernail happens to snap off. But it was ever thus. In the early days of railway travel it was difficult – particularly for those passengers who'd known the coaching days – to understand that stopping a train was not the same as stopping a carriage and four.

Instances are recorded of passengers pulling the communication cord because they'd been sleeping and, having woken with a start, feared they might have missed their station. There are records of passengers stopping the train at the point where it passed closest to their homes rather than wait until it had gone another 3 miles and stopped at the station. There are even records of passengers stopping the train simply because they were fed up with the journey and several instances are recorded of passengers stopping the train to ask that their footwarmers be re-heated. But the prize for the most absurd reason given for stopping a train has to go to an old lady who pulled the communication cord on a non-stop London to Glasgow express. She didn't just pull it – she yanked on it violently and repeatedly and to such an extent that guard, ticket collector and dining room attendant came running. The train screeched to a halt even while they ran through the corridors. But when they got to the old lady's compartment they found nothing amiss – other than an extremely agitated pensioner. What on earth was the matter? The woman waved her umbrella menacingly in the face of the guard and shouted: 'Why didn't you stop before, you fool? We've just passed some of the finest mushrooms I've seen in years!'

FOOTWARMER

ENGLAND, 1863

Express trains and other trains deemed important by various independent railway companies in the nineteenth century were warmed during the winter season by steam, an innovation that, overnight, reduced the need – at least on some journeys – for vast numbers of greatcoats and capes, hats, gloves and scarves.

The steam-heating innovation was a clever one because the steam used to heat the carriages was recycled steam that had already been used to drive the engine. The system was to force the steam along pipes from end to end of the train with connections going into each compartment of the carriages.

Most people loved the new system, which also dispensed with the need for cumbersome and inefficient footwarmers, but a few diehards petitioned for it to be abandoned. Among the latter was an old lady who, prior to taking her seat in a train that was about to leave King's Cross station in London, asked, in a tone that suggested she had no intention of being refused, to be provided with a footwarmer. Since footwarmers were no longer available, she was politely informed that this would not be possible but that she could comfort herself with the knowledge that the carriages were now heated in a far more efficient way by steam.

According to the policeman who was soon called to the scene, she at once assumed an extremely militant attitude, and railed against the new method, apparently for no conceivable reason other than that it was a departure from a practice she had grown accustomed to, and that she could not bear such new-fangled notions.

She demonstrated the full depths of her anger by using an umbrella to poke and swipe at the poor old railwayman who'd originally come along to see if he could help her, which was a bit unfair as he couldn't have supplied her with a footwarmer even if he'd wanted to, since none was available. With the aid of the policeman who calmed her down, the patient railwayman at last persuaded the old lady to at least try sitting for a few moments in one of the steam-heated compartments. She entered, with misgiving written largely on her countenance, and immediately declared that the atmosphere was unbearable, and that she knew beforehand that it would be so.

'But, how can that be,' said the railwayman, 'when the engine is not yet attached to the train, and the steam pipe, which you're welcome to touch, is stone cold?'

Her only answer was to shout at both the railwayman and the attendant policeman:

'Get away with you both. I will in future travel on a line where they will not both boil me and make me make a fool of myself.'

SALT AND PEPPER

ENGLAND, 1863

Mr Salt was one of a group of railway traffic officers who first promoted the idea of the railway companies organising and bidding for their own freight-carrying contracts.

Before Mr Salt arrived on the scene, middle men, such as Carver & Co., Weavers, Crowley and the famous firm of Pickfords, who had been carriers by road and canal, dominated the trade and passed on to the rail only those bits of business they either didn't want themselves or couldn't cope with.

In addition to Mr Salt, the Midland Railway, quite by chance, employed a Leeds-based manager called Mr Pepper and at various railway meetings of the day there were endless jokes as to Pepper and Salt being mustered.

The sherry and sandwich luncheons were incomplete without the appearance of these two condiments. Mr Salt was a man with a very cadaverous countenance and he'd first been employed by the railway as a scarer. Before the days when compartments could be reserved, this was vital if the railway's own officials were not to be disturbed by ordinary members of the pubic while travelling on their own railway. The permanently ill-looking Mr Salt was ordered to tie up his head with a handkerchief, and sit gloomily by a window. Few ventured to enter where such evidence existed of a fellow passenger at the point of death.

UNHEALTHY JOURNEY

ENGLAND, 1863

Having researched the subject at great length and based on the best scientific advice available, Dr Walter Lewis, the medical officer of the London Post Office, travelled across England by train in 1863, to try to understand the effects of railway travel on humans.

Following his lengthy journey, he issued his report and concluded that 'railway travel has little, if any, injurious effect on healthy, strong, well-built persons, if the amount be not excessive, and if they take moderate care of themselves.'

But, after being shaken about on his own journey, he concluded that 'persons who take to habitual railway travelling after the age of 25 or 30 are more likely to suffer internal convulsions and potential damage to bodily organs than those who begin earlier, and the more advanced in age a traveller is, the more easily is he affected by this sort of locomotion. Weak, tall, loosely-knit persons, and those suffering under various affections, more especially of the head, heart, and lungs are very unsuited for habitual railway travelling.'

LUGGAGE ON THE ROOF

SCOTLAND, 1865

In the early days of the railway, conductors were in charge of all passenger trains to Scotland. They were senior to ordinary guards and at first they were given the job of travelling on trains between London and Glasgow, but, in 1865, through a joint recommendation between the Scottish Central Railway and the Caledonian Railway, it was agreed they should also travel between Euston and Perth.

While the ordinary guards were responsible for the brake vans, the conductor was given special responsibility for the luggage, and in early days had to complete a form for every package. The smartest guards were generally selected as conductors. A Mr Preston, who ended his career as stationmaster at Carlisle, had, in his youth, been one of these conductors and he had some extraordinary tales of the perils of travelling with luggage on the roof.

The system was to strap the luggage down under heavy tarpaulins, but this did not always guarantee that one's luggage would arrive safely at one's destination – far from it, in fact. On a single never-to-be-forgotten journey Mr Preston remembered watching in horror as one carriage roof-load of luggage was knocked off by a low bridge; then as they went round a long slow bend three large trunks slid from the roof into a muddy field by the side of the tracks. Towards the end of the journey two carriage roofs were set on fire when sparks from the engine ignited the tarpaulins. It was sheer good luck that the light from the flames was noticed in time for the train to stop and the fire to be out before any lasting damage was done.

Mr Preston is recorded as saying:

> I had the satisfaction of seeing this roofing of luggage, a relic of old coaching days, gradually but entirely dispensed with, the manager agreeing to my recommendation to adopt the plan of a separate luggage compartment in the centre of the passenger carriages.

SUNDAY SCHOOL ROBBER

AMERICA, 1866

America's earliest train robbery occurred at Seymour, Indiana. It was an extraordinary robbery in two respects – first because, despite the wild lawlessness of the western United States at the time, no train robbery had ever occurred before and, second, because the man behind the felony was a religious leader and Sunday school teacher!

His name was John T Chapman, a respected resident of Reno. Tall and slender, in his late thirties, he had an angelic expression. Unfortunately his expression changed a great deal whenever he thought about the gold rush at nearby Comstock Lode, which was daily disgorging vast riches of gold and silver ore, creating multimillion-dollar fortunes. Chapman, like many others who were only onlookers at this bonanza, longed for some share in the wealth. However, if he wanted a haul of gold he knew the best way to get it was to concentrate on the trains that hauled the stuff away from the mine.

As time went on, Chapman took closer note of these operations. He then persuaded six friends to come in with him on a daring operation to rob a gold train. Time and place were set, after consideration and careful planning, for the late night of 5 November 1866, near a large rock quarry close to the town of Verdi, then a rugged logging community 11 miles west of bustling Reno.

On the morning before the robbery, R A Jones, a member of the gang, inquired at the desk of the Capitol House in Reno and was handed a telegram from San Francisco. He scanned its lines with a furtive grin. The message read: 'Send me 60 and charge to the account of J Enrique.' This was a code that confirmed that the gold

118

was to leave by train the next day and that the bandits would have six men to contend with in robbing the express car.

Jones passed the word to his associates and final preparations were soon underway. They took their horses and ammunition and rode separately to their selected rendezvous, an old mine tunnel. They spent the day and evening mapping final plans, for the train, they knew, was not due until midnight. Two hours before train time, they put on their gun belts and rode in the moonlight to a nearby station where they would board the train and ride as far as a certain culvert, the exact spot chosen for the hold-up.

The train, with its ornate wood-burning engine painted bright red, puffed its way into the station and stopped to take on a few items of freight. Standing alone on the station platform, the conductor watched as the last crate was lifted aboard. As the wheels started, he swung onto the steps of a coach. Looking ahead at that moment, he was surprised to see the figures of three men climbing aboard the front platform of a baggage car, which was directly behind the express. The conductor, whose name was Marshall, thought they were tramps and he hurried through the carriage, intending to order them off before the train had picked up speed.

The three meanwhile had made their way back through the luggage van to its front platform. As Marshall stepped out on to the platform he found himself staring into the muzzles of revolvers held by masked men. 'Get back in there,' one of them commanded.

The conductor backed away into the van, losing sight of the armed men for a few seconds. In that instant he decided to take the risk of pulling the bell cord that would signal the engineer to stop, but found that the bandits had already cut the cord. Yet, to his surprise, the train suddenly slowed down anyway and almost immediately came to a complete stop. Returning to the open platform at the end of the van Marshall leaned out and saw two of the same bandits on the ground, edging their way between two carriages. What he did not know then was that two more men had crept silently over the tender, piled high with split logs, jumped into the cab, and forced the driver to stop. 'We're cutting you and the first carriages from the train,' they told him.

Marshall could hear heavy pounding and realised that someone was already at work trying to uncouple the carriages. Any resistance would be folly with a gun levelled at his head. So his thoughts turned to the danger facing the passenger coaches if their brakes were not applied, since the train was on a gradient. Once the engine had been de-coupled there would be nothing to stop the carriages rolling away down the hill. Then he felt a sharp forward lurch, and the driver realised that the work of uncoupling the carriages had been done.

'Now run your engine and the carriages away,' one of the gunmen commanded. 'We'll tell you where to stop.'

The driver, sitting beside his fireman, realised the danger of the situation. Speaking calmly despite the risks he knew he faced, he pointed out that the rest of the train was on a gradient and that he must signal the crew to set the handbrakes or the uncoupled passenger cars would come rolling toward them and finally crash into them.

'We'll handle that,' the taller of the bandits snapped, but the driver was not to be deterred from doing his duty. He whistled the signal to apply the brakes and the guard further back in the train knew what to do. The armed pair swore angrily, warning against any further disobedience. 'Now get moving,' they ordered, and the driver ran his engine and the first of the carriages to the quarry, only a short distance away. There he was told to stop and his eyes, following the beam of the locomotive light, saw close to the tracks a lone man and half a dozen saddled horses.

Driver and fireman were ordered to leave the cab and climb down, followed by the bandits still pointing their guns. Driver and fireman were told to stand aside and remain quiet. One of the gunmen kept them covered while the other began dragging pieces of timber from the roadside, and dropping them across the tracks to stop the coaches should they get out of control and roll down the hill.

Then, as the driver and his fireman looked on, they saw three men with guns running to the door of the carriage containing the gold. 'Open up and come out,' one of them called. 'Do as we tell you.' A moment later the driver saw the carriage door slide open and the staff jumped clear. The man guarding the driver and fireman then directed them to walk to the narrow mail compartment, which was then locked.

Then came loud sounds of hammering as the robbers broke into the boxes filled with gold. The gold was loaded on to horses and minutes later the American West's first train robbery was over.

In the weeks that followed, FBI agents kept an eye on the gambling dens of Reno, where it was soon obvious that the tall Sunday school teacher had suddenly come into a great deal of money.

Before long six men had been identified as being too rich for their own good. They were arrested and soon began to implicate each other. Some of the gold was recovered but most was hidden away in shallow holes dug out in the desert. Each of the men was sentenced to twenty years in prison but much of their gold was never recovered and still lies hidden where it was buried all those years ago.

MAD DOCTOR

AMERICA, 1866

A businessman based in New York received a letter from his solicitor just before Christmas inviting him to a very important meeting in Chicago. 'If you don't attend you may miss something that could be enormously to your advantage,' said the letter. The businessman decided to make the trip. He travelled on 23 December and, rushing to the station through the snow on the morning of that day, found he'd missed the train he intended to catch and had to wait several hours for the next.

At last he boarded the train and made himself comfortable in a first-class carriage, in which there was only one occupant beside himself. This was a little man, well dressed but with disordered hair and what the businessman later described as a curiously glittering and restless look in his eyes. As soon as the businessman had settled in his fellow traveller spoke.

'A merry Christmas to you!'

'The same to you,' said the businessman.

'Why bless me,' said the little old man, 'you haven't anything to keep you warm on this bitter day. Allow me to offer you one of my travelling wrappers.' With that he took from his side a rolled up rug, unrolled it and, taking a small mahogany box from inside it, threw the rug to his companion.

The businessman thanked the stranger and settled down to read his paper.

'I like to have a comfortable face opposite me,' said the old man.

'Why's that?' said the businessman.

'Why, the grand experiment you know,' came the reply.

'What grand experiment?'

'Oh nothing, nothing.'

'Are you a freemason?' asked the old man.

'No I am not,' came the slightly irritated reply.

'Well you should be,' said the old man. 'Because you would then know that they have a sort of secret.'

'Well I knew that already,' said the businessman.

'Really,' came the reply. 'Well you are the most extraordinary man. I have a secret too and that's my grand experiment.'

'Well as it's a secret I suppose you won't tell me what it is.'

'Oh I will. It is simply to discover what are the different feelings of different persons on different occasions.'

'I should hardly call that an experiment.'

'Wouldn't you,' came the reply, 'well to tell you the truth I don't know myself whether I'm quite justified in calling it an experiment. But enough of that. May I ask where you are travelling to?'

'Chicago.'

'You have friends there?'

'None, I'm afraid.'

'Then may I have the pleasure of your company at dinner when we arrive there?'

'But of course.'

The businessman and his eccentric companion then fell silent. Ten minutes later the silence was broken by the little man.

'Do you know how many times we stop before we reach Chicago?'

'Only twice, as this is the express: at 2 o'clock and then again at 5. We should arrive at Chicago at 6.30.'

'Thank you,' said the old man, who seemed to be taking notes.

Soon the businessman fell asleep but his dreams were troubled. First he dreamed he was being hanged; then he dreamed he was being handcuffed and that a great weight was pressing on his chest. He then woke with a start to find himself bound hand and foot with a rope passed round his neck and tied to an umbrella stand in such a way that any struggling would begin to throttle him.

The little old man was now standing over the businessman with his knee pressed firmly into his chest.

'Now I shall be able to try my grand experiment,' said the little old man, 'Now I will be able to see if the heart can be extracted while a man is alive without killing him. Twice I have failed but the stars tell me that I shall not fail a third time.'

Then, addressing the businessman directly, he said:

'If you die you will die a glorious martyr. If you live, you and I will share the glory of this great discovery!'

The businessman could do nothing – he could not struggle and a gag prevented him shouting for help. Then the old man opened his mahogany case to reveal a set of extremely sharp-looking surgical instruments. The businessman tried desperately to remember how soon they were due at their first stop – that was his only chance of being saved.

Frozen by terror, the businessman could only watch as the old man prepared his knives and his victim. He tore open the businessman's shirt and waistcoat. He sharpened several fearsome-looking instruments. At last everything seemed to be ready to the maniac's satisfaction and he picked up a razor-sharp scalpel. The businessman, eyes agog, hardly dared to breathe. The old man tested the knife on the back of his hand. It barely touched the skin but the skin parted in a red wave. The old man pressed his finger to the businessman's chest just where the heart would be and said: 'This is how I'm going to manage it, my friend. I am going to cut a circle in the flesh in the vicinity of the heart with this knife. It will not hurt much as I intend to cut only through the skin. I will then use this,' he waved another fearsome instrument in the air, 'to dig out the heart.'

The businessman said later that he wanted only to scream at this point but the gag prevented it.

The old man cut through the skin and drew his bloody circle, but the businessman – despite his terror and pain – noticed that the train was slowing down. The old man was so intent on his work that he didn't notice. Just as he finished cutting the circle through the upper layers of skin the lights of the station flashed through the windows and, in the next confused minutes, a strange arm appeared as if from nowhere and pulled the old man away. A scuffle ensued and there was shouting and arguing, but beyond that nothing. The businessman was unconscious.

For two weeks the businessman was in a life-threatening fever, but when he recovered he learned that his assailant had once been a doctor and a surgeon. As a young man he'd married, only to discover that his wife had cancer. He had operated, but the young woman died anyway. The surgeon became insane and had been committed to a mental hospital. For decades he had tried to escape in order to perform the operation that had nearly killed the businessman on the train.

THREE TRAINS COLLIDE

ENGLAND, 1866

One of the strangest and most dreadful railway accidents happened at Welwyn in Hertfordshire in 1866. It seems almost incredible that three trains should crash into each other in a tunnel and catch fire, and that the tunnel should be left for hours a huge furnace, with flames vomiting from its mouths and leaping up through 50 feet of rock, to pour from the air-shaft in such volume as to redden the sky – but that's exactly what happened.

Welwyn is, or was, on the Great Northern Line, between Hatfield and Stevenage, leaving it about a mile to the left. There was first a tunnel, a quarter of a mile long, known as the South Welwyn, then a deep cutting a quarter of a mile long, then a tunnel three-quarters of a mile long, known as the North Welwyn. The underlying geology was, and is, chalk, but just on the top of the two tunnels were spurs of much harder rock. The harder rock forms a thin layer, but the bulk of the 50 feet from the crown of the tunnel arch to the top of the shaft of the North Welwyn rose almost entirely through chalk.

A few minutes after midnight on Saturday, 9 June 1866, there ran into the south end of this tunnel a train of 38 empty coal-wagons, on its way to Hitchin. With the train were the engine driver and fireman, and a guard named Wray, who had in his brake van, unknown to the others, a friend named Rawlins, to whom he was secretly giving a lift. The friend was in the brake van against all the rules – something for which both men would pay dearly.

All went well with the empty freight train until it reached the middle of the North Tunnel, just under the air-shaft, when one of the tubes from the boiler burst, and so weakened the power of the engine so that it could not draw the load. The driver, a man called Sizer, sent his fireman, John Kemp, to explain to Wray the reason for the stoppage, and tell him to go back to the south end of the tunnel and give the alarm. This, however, the guard refused to do. On the contrary, he suggested, as they were on an incline, that the train should be backed down the slope out of the tunnel. To go back on the wrong line is against all the rules of railway management, and so the driver refused to do anything of the sort.

His plan, by contrast, was to uncouple the engine, which was powerful enough to run by itself and, leaving the trucks, make all haste on to Stevenage for assistance. It so happened that the signalman at the south end of the tunnel had advised the signalman at the north end that the train was due. The south end signalman waited for some time and then telegraphed his colleague at the other end of the tunnel to try to find out if the train had passed out, as another one was due. The signalman at the north end wired back that the train had not passed out, but the south man read the 'No' as a 'Yes', and shifted the signals to 'all clear'. The down Midland goods train, of 26 heavily loaded trucks, came along as he did so, and the driver saw the signals change from red to white, to give him a clear run. He dashed on into the tunnel.

Kemp, the fireman on the stopped train, had just uncoupled the crippled engine when the Midland goods train slammed into the guard's van and sent the empty trucks flying off the line. Wray and the stowaway, being at the back of the stalled train, were killed instantly. The engine was derailed, and the trucks were thrown over on to the up line and piled up in heaps against the crown of the arch.

With extraordinarily good luck, the driver and fireman were not killed; they escaped, though they were deeply shocked. Indeed, as if to make a moral point, the only lives lost in the whole affair were those of the rule-breaking guard and his friend. No sooner had Sizer and Kemp felt the bump of the collision in the rear of their long train, than an up train roared past them. This was the Scottish meat train on its way to London. In a second it had ploughed at top speed into the wagons already piled up to the roof of the tunnel from the earlier collision. The engine dug deep into the wreckage of the other trains and added to it its own.

Miraculously, the driver and fireman were thrown clear of the wreckage. But this time the fire from the engine had ignited the oil flowing from the barrels with which the Midland train had been loaded, and flames broke out. The Midland driver and fireman ran to the south end of the tunnel; the Northern driver went off on the damaged engine to Stevenage, and the Scottish driver and fireman retreated in the same direction from the suffocating smoke and heat. Thirty-six carriages were on fire. With the draughts from either end of the tunnel and the tightly enclosed mass of combustible material the whole thing quickly became a furnace.

The flames mounted the airshaft, shooting with a deafening roar hundreds of feet into the air, and from the tunnel ends streaks of fierce flame occasionally scorched through the rolling billows of thick black smoke.

Help came, but nothing could be done. The heat was intense. The explosions of the cases and barrels carried into the tunnel on the goods train could be heard for miles around. All that could be done was to let the fire burn itself out. Meanwhile, navvies were attempting to clear the line, and 450 stood ready to begin as soon as the fire permitted. Then the Marquis of Salisbury sent his personal fire engine from Hatfield House, and this was run into the tunnel. But where was the water to come from? Amid deafening whistling and screaming, engines came backing in with their tenders full, from which the fire-pumps were fed. As one tender was emptied it was run out to make room for another, and from tender to tender the pipe was passed, while the navvies, in gangs of fourteen, took turns at the pumps. Slowly the fire was quenched.

At the bottom of the air-shaft it burst out again, and again more tenders were backed in, and the whole process of drowning the fire began again. Then the tenders were taken out, and cranes mounted on wagons were run in. Huge chains were wound round the burnt wreckage and, bit by bit, sometimes in small masses, sometimes in huge tangled masses, the heap of black, smouldering half-molten twisted metal was dragged out of the tunnel. Often two engines would come puffing out of the tunnel dragging behind them a huge catch of ironwork and charred wood. Each massive bundle seemed to consist only of springs and bolts, nuts and rails, telegraph wire and wheels, screws and crowbars, coke, coal, baked meat, wheat and flour, all jumbled up together. It was more like clearing a choked sewer than a railway. What could be unhitched or unscrewed was unhitched or unscrewed. What had to be broken up was broken up. What could not be got apart was dragged out wholesale, scraping against the sides and crown of the tunnel, and tearing up the ballast beneath the tracks.

The three trains had choked the tunnel for hundreds of yards and, as two of them were heavily loaded with goods, the wreckage formed in places almost a solid plug. Again and again the flames were rekindled by the air from the ventilation shafts and by 12.30 on Sunday morning the county police thought they had discovered a volcano. Soon, from all quarters of the thinly populated district the people were attracted to the light.

As the day broke and the fire sank for the last time the crowds gathered in silence at the tunnel ends. Yard by yard the wreckage was cleared away and, over the ruined engines, the gangs from each end met. Then the tough job of taking away the engines piecemeal began, and with the coming of Sunday night the line was clear and the clouds dispersed.

FARE DODGERS

ENGLAND, 1867

Despite the huge numbers of staff employed to check these things, the first decades of passenger rail services were plagued by ingenious passengers finding ways to avoid paying their fares. Ticket collectors and inspectors were everywhere; tickets were checked on the train, perhaps twice in the same journey, and at the barrier.

But still the crafty managed to slip by and, in the 1860s, it was estimated that losses to the railway companies from people avoiding paying for their tickets ran into tens of thousands of pounds each year – in today's money that would translate into several millions.

The various railway companies tried all sorts of methods to reduce this kind of fraud, but as fast as they came up with new systems the fraudsters found ways to avoid them.

One scam, uncovered on the London to Brighton line in 1867, must count as the most extraordinary ever devised to avoid paying fares. The sharp-eyed inspector who uncovered the scam had noticed that every morning on the busy up train a rather thin-faced woman in huge mid-Victorian-looking skirts lumbered slowly on to the train and came back two hours later on the down train looking somehow less lumbering.

Something about the woman was odd but the inspector at first couldn't work out what it was. Then he began to notice that she travelled rather a lot but never seemed to go anywhere – or at least, having travelled on the up train she was back on the next, or nearly next, down train. She was out and back so quickly that she could

130

never have time to do anything in between times. So what on earth was the point of her continual journeying?

It was only when the woman tripped as she boarded a train one winter's morning that the inspector realised what was going on. As she stumbled the inspector noticed two pairs of small feet poking out of her voluminous skirts – that is, two pairs in addition to the woman's own feet. The inspector was astounded, but given the proprieties of the age he could do nothing – the idea of walking up to the woman and lifting her skirts was unthinkable. But the inspector bided his time. He let her get on the train and continue her journey. He let her come back as she usually did on the next down train. But the next morning when she arrived at the station the inspector was waiting with two female detectives. They escorted the woman into a waiting room and discovered two four-year-olds under her voluminous bustle and skirts. They were dressed in school uniform and were being taken each day to their kindergarten by the woman. The woman later confessed that she was paid a small sum each day by the children's parents – a sum considerably less than the real fare – and was able to travel free herself as the widow of a former driver. She was fined two guineas and warned that she might go to prison if she was ever caught doing it again.

GUNPOWDER CRASH

ENGLAND, 1867

A bizarre railway accident happened near Penrith, in Cumberland, in 1867. The London and North Western Railway, on its way from Lancaster to Carlisle along the very edge of the Lake District, runs through Tebay junction, Shap, famous for its granite, and Clifton, and then reaches Penrith, where tourists change for Keswick. It was along this lonely rocky line, at about 11.20 on the night of 26 February, that a goods train, having successfully climbed the Shap incline, went puffing through Clifton in that slow heavy way peculiar to goods trains.

Amid the noise, the axle of one of the wagons broke, but neither the driver nor guard were aware of the breakdown. On went the goods train, puffing hard in the darkness, a long string of trucks with miscellaneous cargoes, some laden with salt, one laden with gunpowder. Suddenly the truck with the broken axle slipped off the rails. Before the driver could stop, another truck followed suit, then another, then another; and as the engine slowed, the trucks towards the end of the train ran closer and forced the forward ones across on to the up line.

As luck would have it, the wagon filled with 4 tons of gunpowder came to a halt slap bang in the middle of the up line. Before the men in charge could do anything to give notice of the danger they heard the roar of an approaching train on the up line. It was another goods train. The driver of that train, seeing no signal, and supposing the line clear, came along at full speed – straight into the gunpowder wagon. Instantly, there was a shower of sparks and a vast all-encompassing explosion that shook and rumbled hundreds of feet into the air and deep down into the earth.

A searing burst of flame shot up and lit the whole district. The explosion shook even the distant hills; the earth trembled as if from the shock of an earthquake. For 4 miles round about the windows of farmhouses were smashed; and for 20 miles round the roar was clearly audible. The driver and stoker were killed; the wagons and goods hurled about in all directions. From the engine fires the wagons caught light, and they burnt for hours, the heavy smoke cloud hanging over the blaze and glowing red with its reflection.

As soon as they had recovered from their terror the four survivors – the driver and fireman of the train from the south, and the guards of both trains – took measures to stop the traffic north and south of the blockage. The explosion had occurred close to Yanwath Bridge. From there to Penrith is but a mile or so. The breakdown gang were soon on the spot, and by 7 o'clock the next morning the line was clear, but the wreckage piled by the side was left to burn itself out, and it took all day to do so.

ANIMAL MAGIC

ENGLAND, 1868

The rules for railway travel had to adapt according to circumstances and changes in expectations. However, as the rules developed, the problem was often that they did not always keep ahead of the realities of rail travel. Thus the business of insisting that dogs had to be paid for as if they were human passengers could lead to some absurd situations.

A London and North Western passenger guard once got himself into a terrible tangle over the rules concerning dogs and tickets. At Manchester, a collie bitch, booked for Bethesda, was placed in his charge, but by the time Chester was reached the bitch had given birth to two puppies. At Chester a consultation was held by the railwaymen, and it was decided – railwaymen traditionally being soft-hearted and sympathetic characters – to make a bed for the mother and puppies on the station premises. With some difficulty the little family was removed and put in comfortable quarters, and three more puppies were added to the number in due course.

But now came the problem of tickets. One dog had been paid for and now there were five puppies and the original dog. Who was to pay for the extra individuals? The guard and stationmaster consulted the massive rule book (in Victorian times this was the railwayman's bible and, in theory at least, it covered every eventuality). This particular eventuality, however, had not been covered, or at least not in the history of the London and North Western. What on earth was to be done?

The enlarged consignment could not be put on the next train until the matter was resolved. Discussions were held while the mother was provided with nourishment in her comfortable bed. Officials gathered and agendas were written out for various meetings. At last a decision was reached. The mother and her puppies were forwarded as soon as it was felt the puppies could manage the journey, the carriers and the consignee having the unusual satisfaction of delivering and receiving respectively six times the number of animals shown on the way-bill. The collie was a well-bred animal, and the puppies were described as '11 beauties'.

But how was the ticket problem resolved? Well, a special leather wallet had been made at Chester and in it were placed eleven half-fare tickets with a note requesting payment from the dog's owner should he deem this 'acceptable in the general spirit and goodwill of travel'. The wallet also contained a note explaining how the collie had been looked after immediately following delivery. It was then attached to the collie's collar. History does not record if the dog's owner decided that, in a spirit of fair play, he or she should pay up.

ANTI-SMOKING

ENGLAND, 1868

The idea that anti-smoking legislation is a modern obsession is entirely wrong, or at least it is if we are to judge by the mid-Victorian directors of the Great Western Railway (GWR). They hated smoking in their trains and even in their stations. They were especially active in enforcing the by-laws prohibiting it, and prosecuting offenders.

In June 1865, the General Manager of the GWR issued special orders that no smoking was to be allowed anywhere on the company's premises under any circumstances whatever. But then, to the disgust of the GWR directors, parliament passed a law that obliged the railway companies to provide smoking carriages on their trains. This came into force on 1 October 1868. Obliged to comply, a Mr Grierson, one of the most senior and exalted of all GWR officials, ordered that only the end compartments of the carriages near the rear of the train should be designated for smoking, and as few of them as possible, and that smoking should still be rigorously prevented in the stations, goods yards and everywhere else.

Staff and passengers were outraged and on one particular occasion there was a smoking protest. A hundred or more passengers – apparently unconnected with each other – clambered abroad an express and largely occupied three carriages at the front of the train where smoking was strictly forbidden.

They proceeded to smoke their pipes and cigars far more vigorously than they would ever do under normal circumstances.

The guard found he was overwhelmed by the number of smokers, all of whom had to be ejected at the next station. Umbrellas were brandished, loud arguments ensued, the guard was at times surrounded by a sea of angry puffers and the train almost had to be taken out of service. Indeed, when it stopped at a small country station the platform porter noticed more smoke coming from the windows of the carriages than from the engine.

At last the police were called and order was restored but the smokers had made their point and, as the years went by, smoking came to dominate trains with, by the 1950s, just one or two carriages per train designated non-smoking.

BATTLE OF THE NAVVIES

ENGLAND, 1869

Britain's roads, railways and canals are mostly the work of Irish navvies. In the days of Ireland's greatest poverty – the middle decades of the nineteenth century – almost everyone who could raise the boat fare left for England or America or Australia. Those who came to England found work in their thousands first on the canals and then later on the railways.

But conditions were extraordinarily harsh. Navvies worked from dawn till dusk in summer and often in remote regions where there was nowhere to stay at night and no food to be had round about. The railway companies took no notice whatsoever of the navvies' difficulties, arguing, as one railway director put it, that 'We may have to pay them, a nuisance in itself as they are ruffians to a man, but we are not also obliged to ensure they have a life of comfort and ease that would risk arousing in them an envy of their betters.'

So the navvies slept by the tracks under tarpaulins and in tool sheds or even out in the open, night after night for months on end. This turned them not into a race of wild men but certainly into a fearsome tribe – which may explain why it was frequently necessary for the cavalry to be called when the navvies began fighting with each other or with other groups of navvies they met along the tracks.

The biggest navvy battle of them all occurred in the 1860s, when a large group of Irish navvies began work on a section of railway that had inadvertently been scheduled to be worked by another group of English navvies. The two groups soon came to blows and even the local militia could do little to stop the bloodletting: at the end of the day the Irish had routed the English but many on both sides were seriously injured, one lay dead and at least fifty were carted off to prison. The incident did little to dispel the view held by traditionalists and the landed gentry that wherever the railway went trouble was sure to follow.

NARROW ESCAPE FOR DICKENS

IRELAND, 1868

Charles Dickens seems to have had a knack for getting himself into scrapes with railway trains. Most famously he narrowly escaped death in the Staplehurst accident – a bizarre incident in which the identity of the woman with whom he was travelling was never discovered – but during a remarkable journey through Ireland by train the great novelist almost met his end again.

Percy Fitzgerald, a contributor to the Irish newspaper *TP's Weekly*, recalled the start of what turned out to be an almost disastrous day:

> Once at the railway station in Belfast – it was in the morning, and I was travelling with the great man – there was a little incident that got the day off to a bad start. Of course, his figure always excited a good deal of attention; everyone knew him from the prints or description. He was always quite unconcerned at the staring and whispering. He was so unaffected; he behaved just as though he were alone. I see him as the stationmaster comes up obsequiously to make a request. We had noted a smug, burly man in a white waistcoat and heavy gold chain, who was standing by smiling on us with affability. It was he who had deputed the stationmaster. The white waist-coated man was one of the great local flax-spinners. He would like, he said – if Mr Dickens had no objection – to join him in his coupé for the journey.

Fitzgerald tells us that Dickens apparently looked panic-stricken and, after making what was by all accounts a very polite refusal, he vanished into a coupé carriage and begged that the journey might start as soon as possible. Dickens' haste to be gone may have reduced the amount of time available for the proper checks to be made on the mechanics of the train by the wheel tappers and others, but whether or not that was the case it's certainly true – as events were soon to demonstrate – that the engine at least was in a poor condition.

The accident that was to come was made worse by the fact that Dickens was travelling in a coupé carriage. The coupé carriage, the last examples of which vanished more than a century ago, was extraordinarily luxurious and fitted with a specially made front that was constructed almost entirely of plate glass in order that VIPs should be able to get the best possible view during the journey. Railway travel of any kind was such an adventure in the middle decades of the nineteenth century that there was demand for a carriage that would allow the full pleasure of travelling at speed to be enjoyed.

So there was Dickens relaxing in his coupé when the engine set off on the Belfast and Newry line. As the train reached a good straight stretch of track, the driver increased his speed and the massive tyre of the driving wheel on the engine broke into huge fragments, one of which smashed into the coupé window – missing Dickens by inches. A newspaper reporter later said that Dickens' escape without a scratch was nothing less than miraculous.

SHOOTING
FROM THE TRAIN

ENGLAND, 1870

An eccentric Victorian landowner was very keen on shooting but hated all the walking involved between drives. The problem was particularly acute on his estate as the drives were some distance from each other. He tried travelling by horse; he even tried paying four of his servants extra for carrying him round in a sedan chair. This was fine but it was difficult to shoot from the chair itself, which was what he really wanted, so the experiment was abandoned. Horses tended to bolt at the first bang.

Early bicycles seemed to hold out the prospect of shoot travel of the highest order, but by the time he'd ordered one of the new-fangled – and very expensive – machines, the duke realised that it would be little use over rough terrain needing smooth tarmac to work properly.

The duke's hatred of travel meant that when bicycles and horses and sedan chairs failed he tried all sorts of schemes to ensure that rather than his having to travel to the birds the birds would travel to him. He planted woods near the house and had the pheasants driven towards the terrace, where he would sit ready to shoot. He even thought that if it worked well he would sit inside the house by the drawing room window and shoot the birds as they flew over. The crafty old pheasants were too clever to fall for that one. Most simply ran across the lawns and round the house.

Eventually he had a brainwave. If the pheasants wouldn't come to his seat he would take his seat to the birds. He called in the leading surveyors and engineers and had a miniature railway built, complete with open carriages. He learned to drive the train and persuaded the bemused engineers to build the track so it ran from one drive to the next, even taking in odd bits of woodland on the edges of the estate that would be used only occasionally. The result was a great success. The duke had little branch lines built so he could drive in and out of dead ends and he made sure that, ultimately, if he went far enough on his railway, he would get back to where he started. He built other branch lines off the main circuit so he could examine his pens.

After the railway had been completed the great day arrived – the first day of the shooting season. The duke went down to the platform at the front of the house and boarded his little train. At the first drive he shot as he'd always wished from a specially built seat at the back of the engine. He did very well and enjoyed good sport at all the subsequent drives. He wrote to his friends and invited them to come and try his new shoot. They came and were each accommodated in a small, individual carriage that was then attached to the engine where the duke himself always sat. It was, as he was to observe on many occasions, the triumph of art over nature.

MUSHROOMS IN THE TUNNEL

SCOTLAND, 1870

Victorian travellers heading along the last mile of tunnel into Edinburgh Waverley would have been astonished to be told that shortly after a new detour to the east necessitated the abandoning of the old tunnel, extensive mushroom beds were established by the side of the track. In the dim, damp conditions this produced an extraordinarily profitable business.

The old North British Railways tunnel got into Waverley by a tunnel under St Andrews Square and Princes Street. It was about three-quarters of a mile long and so steep that the engineers had to build a stationary steam engine to help drag the locomotives up the incline. Once an alternative route had been established, the tunnel and stationary engine fell into disuse.

Then someone approached the railway company with the idea of growing mushrooms in the tunnel. The railway company were not too exacting about terms as they knew they would be paid to carry the materials for the hotbeds in and the mushrooms out.

A visitor one cold March morning found a huge fire of anthracite burning just inside the lower mouth of the tunnel. In this way the chill was taken off the air. What used to be the up line was kept clear for mushroom beds. The down line had an engine on it to carry the workers as well as fertiliser, stock, produce and soil in and out. Conditions in the tunnel were so good from an agricultural point of view that tunnel mushrooms were always on the market each year well before imports from warmer foreign climes.

'THEY'RE AN INSEK'

ENGLAND, 1870

Frank Buckland, the Victorian naturalist, inventor and for many years Chief Inspector of Her Majesty's Fisheries, had a house full of animals. As a boy at Winchester school he kept hares and frogs and tortoises, mice, rats and even eels in a bath. By the time he'd reached middle age he had a house in London filled to bursting with live, dead, caged, uncaged, dying, stuffed and pickled animals from all over the world.

A visitor was as likely to meet a monkey on the stairs or an armadillo as a cat or dog. For years, a dead gorilla languished in a large barrel filled with rum while a giant sun fish sprawled in a vast saucer of formaldehyde. In the basement of the house, Buckland dissected any animal that had died and, generally speaking, he then cooked and ate it. One of his chief claims to fame and legacies to the modern world was the Buckland Dining Club, which still meets today. A typical menu will consist of sea slug followed by dormouse on toast.

But, in addition to his passion for animals of all sorts, Buckland had a passion for new inventions and chief among these was the railway. As often as he was able, Buckland would take the train and of course his favourite pets always accompanied him. This was not a problem if the pet of the moment happened to be a dog or even, at a pinch, a cat. Things were more difficult when, as usually happened, Buckland decided to take one or other of his more exotic charges.

Buckland's most famous journey began, as he later recalled, on a foggy autumn morning when he presented himself at St Pancras station ticket office.

145

Buckland was taking with him on the journey a monkey, which proved a bit of a stumbling block to the booking office clerk, who carefully went through the schedule of charges for the carriage of animals.

'Cows is horses,' at length said the booking office clerk, 'and so is donkeys. Cats is dogs and fowls is likewise and so is monkeys. That 'ere animal will have to go as a dog.'

'And what about this?' said an indignant Buckland, pulling a tortoise out of his pocket.

Once more the schedule was perused.

'They are nothing,' said the clerk with some scorn after a few moments. 'We don't charge nothing for them. They're an insek.'

THE END OF BROAD GAUGE

ENGLAND, 1871

When the Great Western Railway decided at last to adopt the narrow gauge that was standard on the rest of the railway network, the company had to rip up all the old broad-gauge track. They decided to do it on a special one-off journey. The system adopted was to divide the line into lengths of about four miles for each day's work, each length being subdivided into quarter-mile sections, each entrusted to a gang of about twenty platelayers. A long train of broad-gauge vans was provided at the Hereford end of the line, the vans being fitted up with sleeping accommodation for the men, a travelling office for the engineers, blacksmith's shop, stores and temporary kitchens.

At the start of each day this train was worked through the length to be narrowed, stopping every quarter mile to disembark a gang of platelayers with their tools and food for the day, and finally coming to rest at the end of the length. The narrowing was started by each gang first thing in the morning and in about four hours had been completed sufficiently to permit the passing of a narrow-gauge engine very slowly and cautiously driven, over the newly placed rails. Up ahead the last ever broad-gauge train moved over track that would soon be gone forever.

By evening the length was completely finished, packed with ballast and in good running order.

Then commenced the operation of loading up the men and tools into a narrow-gauge train, which carried them forward to the end of the length where the broad-gauge train of vans was awaiting

147

them. Next followed a little miscellaneous cooking, a well-earned supper and an early bed amongst the straw in the vans, in preparation for another day's work, which would start at four o'clock the next morning.

EXTRAORDINARY ESCAPE

AMERICA, 1872

One dark, foggy night, as the express pulled out of Chicago at about 9 o'clock, the guard warned the driver to run slowly through a deep cutting about five miles from the station. 'All right,' he answered, but he was a notoriously fearless driver, who enjoyed nothing in the world better than a swift dash through the roaring tempest, and the guard was worried that he would take no notice of the order.

They got up a good head of speed on the early part of the journey, but the guard was now, if anything, even more worried than before. With the thick fog and the intensely dark night he knew that if there was a problem on the track or if anything went wrong in any other way the driver would have no time to react. And then there was that steep cutting, which always worried him.

The driver began to pick up speed and, though the guard went forward twice to warn him, he seemed unable almost to take any action to slow down. The guard later reported that, in the fog, the whole journey began to take on a dream-like quality – an impression that was strengthened by the curious inability of the driver to do anything other than gradually increase his speed.

As the train reached the steep cutting it was going full pelt, but at least here in the steep-sided ravine the fog had lifted. Then, hardly believing his eyes, the guard saw it – a huge boulder was crashing down the side of the ravine and would almost certainly hit the train. The boulder, which must have been fifteen feet across, seemed to be moving in slow motion and at the speed the train was now travelling there was no way they could stop in time. But

somehow the sense that nothing could be done reconciled the guard
– as he later said – to his fate. There was nothing he could do but
wait for the inevitable collision. Then, as train and boulder were
about to collide, the guard watched in astonishment as the boulder
seemed to hit a ridge about twenty feet above the track and, the jolt
imparted by the ridge, combined with the huge momentum of the
boulder, threw it into the air and clean over the engine. Indeed, there
was a point at which the guard was able to look out the window and
see the massive rock suspended as it were in mid-air above the train.

In later years he always said that the sight of that boulder missing
his train as if by a miracle had almost – but not quite – made him
believe in God.

STEPHENSON'S GAUGE

ENGLAND, 1872

It was in mid-May that the last broad-gauge passenger trains ever to run finished their journeys. It was a Saturday night, 11 May, when the gauge favoured by Stephenson himself finally slipped into the long oblivion of history. The very last broad-gauge train left New Milford at about 9.15pm. A special engine followed the train with inspector Langden aboard and it was his job to distribute notices to all concerned on the route stating that all broad-gauge stock had been removed and would never be used again.

By the Monday, narrow-gauge track had replaced the old line and new trains were carrying passengers along the old route. Despite the fact that the last broad-gauge journey took place in the dark of late evening and night, many gathered to watch a journey that signalled the end of an era and there was a great deal of anger from those who had always believed that the broad gauge was better – because more stable – than narrow.

NOT AMUSED

ENGLAND, 1872

In 1872, the Queen left Windsor on 14 May, accompanied by Prince Leopold and Princess Beatrice, as well as the Marchioness of Ely and Viscount Bridport. The driver had been given special instructions to work his locomotive with the utmost care, particularly when negotiating bends and when slowing down or accelerating.

This had nothing to do with Queen Victoria, who usually loved bowling along at maximum speed. No. It was all down to Prince Leopold. A special saloon, complete with a specially built invalid bed, had been added to the train for him. The Prince was carried into the station on a surgical couch on the back of a horse and cart and then carried by several retainers to the saloon; he was suffering from a slight sprain of the knee but was behaving as if he was a badly injured war hero.

The train arrived safely at Wigan, where it stopped for the night with the passengers sleeping on board. The stationmaster, proud as Punch at the presence of his royal visitors, patrolled along the platform in the dead of night. He did not expect for a minute to see or hear anything of the royal travellers, and was astonished to find John Brown (the Queen's gillie) walking up and down in his kilt and little else, muttering to himself and apparently shouting and barking at phantoms, for no one else was about. The stationmaster asked Mr Brown if everything was all right. Brown roared back: 'No. It isn't all right. I'm checking the wheels. The Queen says the carriage has been shaking like the devil!' And with that he stalked off still cursing and muttering.

When the stationmaster later spoke to the driver he was told that the journey had been as smooth as it was possible for such a journey to be. 'The shaking and racket was probably just Prince Leopold complaining about everything and falling out of bed,' said the driver.

NO JOB FOR A TOFF!

ENGLAND, 1873

The Duke of Buckingham, who also happened to be, among a string of glorious titles, Marquis of Chandos, once applied for a job as a railway porter and was turned down, despite the fact that he was a director of the company!

The man who told the tale was in charge of the station at the time. It was a freezing morning and few people were about. As if from nowhere, a slovenly looking man entered the office and asked if he could see the stationmaster.

'The stationmaster is out,' came the reply. 'I am his deputy.'

'But I wanted to see him,' said the visitor.

'No doubt; but he is out.'

'But I particularly wanted to see him.'

'Yes, many people do; but I know what you want – you want a job – a job on the line. I may at once tell you, you won't do – you're altogether too short for any job, whether porter or guard, and I believe from the look of you that your education is wanting.'

'Perhaps then,' said the stranger, 'You will give the stationmaster my card, and say I should have liked to have seen him.'

The deputy stationmaster looked at the card. It read: 'The Marquis of Chandos.' The deputy stationmaster shook in his shoes, and wondered how soon his dismissal would be announced. He peeked out through the door of his office on to the platform where the marquis was apparently quite contentedly waiting for the next train. So this was the legendary marquis who spent every minute he could travelling by train.

In fact, the marquis was on his way to a very important meeting of the railway company. The Board was to decide who was to become its new chairman – in the event the vacant position was offered to the Marquis of Chandos and accepted by him, his Lordship taking the opportunity of saying that he highly appreciated the compliment of being elected Chairman, though he had just been told, on the good authority of a highly experienced railway official, that he was not fit to be a porter! The deputy stationmaster kept his job.

RUNNING ON WOOD

AMERICA, 1873

The vast natural resources in the United States meant that finding fuel for locomotives was rarely a problem – wherever the trains went, local fuel was usually available in abundance. However, getting the right sort of fuel was sometimes a problem. In some areas, coal was in short supply and, rather than transport the stuff hundreds, perhaps thousands of miles, the railway company owners decided they would build many of their engines to run on wood. The great advantage of this was that across the vast distances of the western United States timber could be harvested all along the route.

This all sounds fine in theory, but as an English visitor to America discovered in 1873 it could have bizarre consequences. He was journeying through a remote region and had been enjoying the splendid view from the window, reading a little and sleeping a great deal, when he noticed that the train was slowing down. Expecting a station he thought no more of it. But then the train stopped dead right in the middle of nowhere he began to wonder what on earth was going on. The Englishman immediately feared a breakdown and worried that he might be stuck in the middle of nowhere for days. But then he heard voices and, looking out of his window, saw the conductor and guard walking along the track shouting up at the passengers, many of whom were already beginning to jump down on to the tracks.

At last, the two railway employees reached the Englishman's part of the train and he heard what they were saying: 'Time to wood up folks!'

It was then that the Englishman realised what was happening. The passengers were collecting wood from a huge woodpile and throwing it into the tender. When he expressed his astonishment to the conductor it was explained that wood was abundant along the route but that since it burned quickly the train had to stop regularly to fill up again with fuel and it was far quicker if all the young strong male passengers gave a hand. If the driver and fireman had to do it all on their own the train might be delayed for several hours.

And thus it continued throughout this part of the Englishman's journey – the train stopped pretty regularly and the passengers happily jumped down and joined the refuelling team.

In England, passengers would have been outraged at the idea of helping out in this way. And even if they had agreed they would expect to be paid for their labour. In America, by contrast, it all seemed to be accepted as part of a pioneering spirit.

GLADSTONE CARRIED AWAY

SCOTLAND, 1873

Punctuality was treated like a religion in some railway companies. The Southern Region was famous for its obsessive desire to ensure trains left and arrived on time and the same was true of the Scottish railway companies. Punctuality took precedence over pretty much everything except safety and even royalty might be left behind if they were a minute late for a train.

One of the most amusing and bizarre examples of this sort of thing occurred at Lockerbie station. Prime minister Gladstone had visited the town and been shown the sights. He'd stayed for several days as part of a lecture tour but was due to leave on the 11 o'clock train for London. Every local worthy from miles round about had gathered to see the great man off: banners were waved, breakfast was laid out on tables on the platform and the mayor and aldermen of the town made lengthy speeches of gratitude.

Gladstone himself was due to give a carefully prepared speech and he stood on the steps of his train ready to deliver it. Unfortunately, the local worthies were queuing up to make their speeches and the last of them simply went on too long. But at last it was Gladstone's turn. He had just begun to speak – standing in the open door of one of his carriages – when the driver of the train looked at his watch, saw it was time to go, knew the rules about being late and set off.

The good citizens of Lockerbie could only stare as the great statesman was carried off, his carefully prepared speech delivered only to the wind. To give him his due, Gladstone did not dive into the safety of his compartment until the train was well out of the station. Presumably he wanted the local people to realise that even though they could not hear his speech he had at least continued to deliver it, apparently oblivious to the fact that every word was lost on the wind.

THE DOG SHOW

ENGLAND, 1875

A clerk who came on duty at the Parcel Office of a Manchester station in the middle of the day had not been long at the counter when a furious passenger appeared there and asked whether a dog that he had previously brought to the office, to be sent to the Liverpool Dog Show, had been despatched to Liverpool by the 11.15am train, as had specifically been requested.

The clerk looked over the entries in his book, and, finding the dog duly entered for the train named, told the passenger that it had been sent. In response the passenger shouted at the top of his voice: 'It's a damned lie!' Somewhat nettled at this outburst, the clerk explained that he could produce the porter who had put the dog into the train, when he was startled by the passenger asking: 'Young man, can you explain how it is that when I got home I found that very same dog you claim to have sent to Liverpool was sitting on my doorstep?'

This appeared so impossible that the clerk immediately dashed off to get the porter who was responsible for putting the dog into the train, and on finding him on the platform, bellowed:

'Oy, Charlie, did you take a dog for the Liverpool Show to the 11.15am?'

'Yes, I did; what about it?'

'Well, there's a gentleman in the office who says that when he got home he found the dog sitting on the doorstep.'

'Did he, now? Well, I'm not surprised.'

'But how could that be if you sent it off by the 11.15?'

'Well, you know, it was like this. When the man brought the dog to the office, it was in a hamper, and he had so much to say about it that Cook (another porter) and I thought we'd like to look at it. So we opened the hamper, and no sooner had we got the lid up than the little beggar jumped out, and bolted through the door, with Cook and I after it as hard as we could go. We followed it down Hunts' Bank and along into Deansgate, where it turned off and went over the bridge into Salford, where, although we did our best to overtake it, we lost sight of it altogether. We looked at each other in dismay, and then, a happy thought occurring to me, I said to Cook, "I'm not going back without a dog. I'll have the first dog I see", and I got a dog and brought it back with me to the station, and that dog's gone to Liverpool.'

Charlie objected very strongly to the proposal that he should repeat this story to the aggrieved customer, but finally agreed to see the sender of the dog, and make a clean breast of it. Fortunately, the humour of the situation appeared to strike the gentleman who, after administering a good-humoured rebuke to the porter, said he would bring the dog back, on a chain, for a later train, and that there was to be no mistake about sending it forward this time.

The sequel to the story is that, on the following day, a hamper containing a dejected-looking dog of uncertain breed was returned to Manchester from Liverpool, with the following endorsement on the label: 'The Secretary of the Liverpool Dog Show declines to exhibit the animal contained herein – cannot classify!'

RUNNING AWAY FROM SCHOOL

ENGLAND, 1875

Charles Scott, who later became a well-known railway engineer, fell in love with the railway system after running away from school. As well as instilling a lifelong passion for railways that early act of rebellion also taught the young Scott a remarkable lesson about the power of the railways and the service they provided.

Scott liked his school, which was in Sherwood near Nottingham, but with his brother – who also attended the school – he one day decided to let on that his mother was ill and that he really ought to go home.

Having explained all this to his best friend, Scott and his brother decided to make a run for home, which was 130 miles away. Scott had managed to save a sovereign, which would be enough, they thought, for the journey, so he and his best friend and his brother began to plan their escape. Late one Wednesday night they dressed in their Sunday clothes, rather than the more conspicuous school uniform normally worn on weekdays, and, at 5am, they shinned down the drainpipe from their dormitory and headed off at top speed across the fields for Nottingham station where they intended to catch the 6am train for London. As the school was 3 miles from the station that allowed an hour to get there.

The school was situated on a hill about two hundred yards away from the main road, which gradually descended into a valley and then rose again to Alapperley, a hill about a mile off, on the way to Nottingham. Unfortunately the three boys were seen leaving the school by one of the servants, who asked a few awkward questions, but did not stop them. They reached the high road but the conversation with the servant had slowed them down and Scott was afraid they'd miss their train. They were making good time when Scott happened to look back – he saw a man on horseback just emerging from the school lane, and clearly galloping after them. They had a head start of a mile, but there were still three-quarters of a mile to run before they would reach the outskirts of Nottingham, and, unless they could do this, they were certain to be caught.

They ran as fast as they could and managed to reach the first houses on the outskirts of the town just fifty yards ahead of the horseman and at once dived down a narrow alley, which had posts at the entrance to stop horses. At last they had shaken him off – or so they thought. They picked their way through the courts and alleys and back slums of Nottingham, instead of keeping to the direct road. They got to the station at 6.05am, and so missed their train. Worse still, there was no other train until 8 o'clock.

Knowing they were still being hunted they managed to lock themselves in the first-class waiting room, where they consumed their only food – a huge lump of very old Christmas cake. After about half an hour they heard a man trying all the doors of the rooms along the platform and searching the station from end to end. Eventually the man tried to open the first-class waiting room door where the three boys were hiding, but evidently concluded it had been locked up for the night, and had not yet been opened, and so passed on.

At 7.57 am Scott cautiously opened the door and looked out, and, not seeing the enemy, slipped into the booking-office. He bought three second-class tickets for London.

When the train entered the station they made a rush for it and managed to get into a second-class carriage. Then disaster struck – just as they thought they were safe, they saw the man who'd chased them on horseback beginning to search the train, starting at the engine.

At last he reached their carriage and the three boys thought the game was up and they'd be dragged back to school and punished. Nothing, they thought, could save them now – but they hadn't reckoned on the extraordinary power of the railway. The man

163

spotted them and made a rush at Scott's brother, but the boy got his arms wrapped round the leg of the seat, from which no amount of tugging could apparently budge him. The man gave up and turned his attention to Scott, who leapt into the luggage rack. Meanwhile, all around the other passengers were arguing and taking sides. At last the guard, hearing a disturbance, came up and inquired what was the matter.

'These young gentlemen,' said the man, 'have run away from school, and I have been sent to fetch them back.'

'Ah! That's a bad job!' said the guard. 'But let me see, have you got a ticket?'

Scott replied that all three of them had indeed bought tickets.

'Then,' said the guard, 'the company has entered into a contract to take you to London, and it is my duty to see that contract is carried out.'

He then turned to the man from the school and said: 'And do you have a ticket?'

The man spluttered and admitted that he did not.

'In that case,' said the guard, 'I must ask you to get off the train, which is about to be delayed.'

With that, he pushed the man out of the door, shut and locked it. He blew his whistle and the train set off for London. The three boys watched the man receding into the distance, astonished at the power of an apparently simple railway ticket. They were eventually punished when they returned to school but the guard's reaction to their appearance on the train stayed with the young Scott and he grew up with a devotion to the railways that lasted right through his working life.

MAD MANOEUVRES

ENGLAND, 1875

Lecturing at a meeting of the Society of Locomotive Engineers, Sir John Aspinall once told the story of an exciting experience that regularly befell him in the early 1870s, when he was firing on passenger engines for the London and North Western Railway.

When the London expresses ran into Crewe, it was usual to call out an extra engine whenever the load was heavy. This extra engine helped the train along as far as the top of a big incline at Tring. Then it was detached, and the manner of detaching was one that made many a railwayman's hair turn grey. The procedure was as follows: as the train drew near to the signal box at Tring, the fireman of the extra engine climbed over the tender and unhooked his engine from the other. Then, the disengaged extra engine ran over the points just ahead, and backed into a siding, waiting there while the London express ran past, afterwards emerging to return to Crewe in readiness for further work. Meantime, the express never stopped, or even slowed appreciably, and there were always breathless, exciting seconds of suspense while the extra engine ran clear.

There was absolutely no mechanical protection should anything have gone wrong, and such a method of working would be considered completely insane today, yet the extraordinary procedure was carried out day after day for years on end.

AGAINST ALL THE ODDS

ENGLAND, 1876

To travel on the Settle to Carlisle line in the North of England – a line completed in 1876 – is to experience one of the most extraordinary journeys it is possible to make by rail. Not, it must be added, because there is anything inherently remarkable about the engines on this line, their speed or about the other passengers: no, in this case the extraordinary fact is that there is a railway there at all.

The difficulties of building the Settle to Carlisle were, at the time the line was built, virtually insurmountable. Most experts said it simply couldn't be done but they reckoned without the resourcefulness of those early railway engineers.

The Settle to Carlisle line is just over seventy miles long, but it took over seven years to make and cost over three million pounds – which was about twenty times the cost of building a comparable length of line at that time anywhere else in the country.

Difficulties dogged the railway engineers almost from the day the railway was planned. When it was being staked out the chief engineer and his men were snowed in for weeks at the Blea Moor Inn, one of the most remote pubs in Britain. For three weeks the snow fell continuously, until it lay seven-and-a-half feet thick, and it was only by driving a tunnel through the snow to the road that the men, who had been living solely on eggs and bacon, got water from a horse-trough to drink.

The making of the line was a battle, with every inch gained only after a massive struggle. Along its whole length there was not a single level piece of ground big enough to build a house on, and the line's embankments, cuttings and tunnels had to go over, under or through almost every variety of rock known to the geologist.

Along the southern part of the line there is a section through boulder clay, the most unsatisfactory of all materials for the railway engineer – one minute it was a thick soup that had to be removed by bucket, the next it was an unyielding rock. One day it was so hard it took tons of explosive to shift; the next, after heavy rain, it turned to glue.

Further on, the engineers hit the diamond-hard rock of the outlying flank of Whernside, Blea moor, where two thousand men worked long shifts for four years or more on embankment, tunnel and viaduct, the wind being at times so high that the bricklayers could not work, for fear of being blown from the scaffold.

In driving the first opening for a tunnel, only four men were able to work in one place, using the technology then available. But to compensate for this, the tunnellers not only bored from each end, but shafts were dug down from the top, each shaft giving two more faces to work at. At Blea Moor there were seven shafts, some of them of 50 feet and more deep. This meant an opening was made for sixteen gangs of men, working night and day, four of the shafts being eventually left as ventilators. Once the initial tunnel had been opened up, the hole was enlarged sufficiently to allow the arch to be put up in brickwork, the space behind the brickwork being filled in with loose rock. Then the excavation of the tunnel was continued down to the level of the rails, and the sides and floor put in. In all this work, vast amounts of dynamite were used and, as this could not be sent by railway, it had all to be carted from Carlisle or Newcastle at a cost of £200 a ton – a huge sum at the time. It was estimated that 33,000 navvies were employed in total before the Carlisle to Settle was finally complete and the first passengers were able to travel on this most remarkable line. Most knew little or nothing of what had been endured to enable their journey to take place.

A WAITING-ROOM REHEARSAL

ENGLAND, 1878

Odd things happen on railway journeys because travel brings disparate people together and keeps them together long enough – in many cases – for interesting relationships to develop. But it isn't often that the circumstances of late trains and pressing needs brings full-blown theatrical performance to a large station waiting room. There's only one recorded instance of this happening, but it was remembered for decades in the southern region principally because the leading actress involved charmed all the station staff to such an extent that they fell in love with her.

It all began with the appointment of a young man as assistant stationmaster at a large junction station, well enough known on the London to Brighton line. Many of the young man's duties lay inside the offices, while other staff dealt with the incoming and outgoing trains, which arrived pretty regularly throughout the day. But the story comes from the days when stations were fully manned in order that every detail of passenger comfort should be properly attended to. Time and commercial pressures have altered all that and the attitude of that distant time is now far beyond human memory.

The young man's boss – the stationmaster – was a strict Presbyterian, and being in addition an old soldier, he was also a strict disciplinarian. Everything at the station was done according to army principles, but despite – or perhaps because of – the stationmaster's obsession with discipline, he commanded the respect of the rest of the station staff. He also had an excellent memory, and he never forgave a lapse of duty. His reports were frequent, and the details, however trivial, were always insisted upon with the exactitude he had learnt in his previous profession.

The young assistant stationmaster knew about all this at first hand because part of his job was to copy out the old man's reports in duplicate, and when they happened, as they did occasionally, to concern the young man, they did not make pleasant writing or reading. So there was respect for the old man, but at the same time a distinct sense of relief when he went on holiday or disappeared for a few days for some other reason. When this happened the young man was left nominally in charge.

One memorable morning the stationmaster received a telegram to say that his presence was required at the general offices, so after he had given himself the extra washing, combing and brushing up he considered indispensable upon these occasions, and had all the staff in one by one to give them the customary caution whenever he left the station, he departed by the 9.30 express.

There was no other train on the main line, down or up, for two hours, but after that it would be very busy for half an hour for the branch trains, of which there were three, up and down, timed to meet the main line arrivals. Then there was another long interval until the same thing occurred again.

The midday trains came and went in the most satisfactory manner, keeping their time within at least half an hour or so, and after he had seen the last one off, the young man determined to treat himself to a leisurely read of the paper. But just then the telegraph boy put a message into his hand. The telegram read 'From Brooklynge to Hatchford Junction' – Brooklynge was the name of the station that terminated one of the branch lines – 'Mrs Crisp's theatrical company No. 20, booked through from here. Please see to first class accommodation on the up main-line.'

In those days travelling theatrical companies were not the regularly organised and constantly arranged-for matters they are now, and accommodation had to be improvised.

Three carriages were got ready to tack on to the main-line train, which arrived just ten minutes late. But the branch train was twenty minutes overdue already, and the station staff hadn't a clue why it was late nor when it might eventually arrive.

The usual messages of inquiry were sent, and at last the young man received information that the branch-line train had broken down about ten miles from the junction, and help was wanted at once. The only available engine was sent out on a rescue mission. At last the rescue train returned and the disabled train crept into the station.

There were only five first-class carriages on that train, so the young man guessed that the theatrical company would form by far the larger portion of the passengers. He was not long finding out their whereabouts, for, as the train ran up to the platform, a female head was thrust out of one of the windows, and a female voice was heard demanding to see the stationmaster. The young man hurried up at once and got to the carriage door as the train stopped.

'Don't do that,' said the woman. 'Never mind the door. We are going on, of course.'

'I'm afraid not, madam,' said the young man. 'Not for two hours, at least.'

'Two hours,' she gasped, and sank back in her seat. 'What is to be done? What is to be done?'

She was a woman of thirty or forty. It was impossible to tell exactly how old she was. In one light she looked thirty, in another fifty. She had strongly marked features, with large eyes and mouth, and her face was so thickly powdered that layers of dust seemed to drift from her continually.

'What is to be done?' she repeated.

'Make the best of it, I should say,' said a girl's voice from the further end of the carriage.

Someone else shouted 'Let's get out anyhow, if we can't get on.'

'But it is impossible for us now to get to town in time, and think of the consequences,' said the older woman.

'Oh, the consequences are not so very awful. A limited section of the British public will be disappointed, that's all,' said the younger woman.

As she spoke she had come to the door, and stood with both her hands resting on the carriage window. She had a roguish look but was by all accounts very beautiful.

'I've got a bright idea,' she said, turning to the older lady.

'We can't get to town now in time for anything but bed, and so I'll tell you what we'll do.'

She looked at the young assistant stationmaster and said. 'You seem to have some nice big rooms here. Lend us the use of the largest, and we will forgive you and your company all their sins for making us late.'

The young man said both he and the railway company would be delighted to be of any service. He also explained how the accident had occurred, and why it was impossible to help the delay. Then the whole company got off the train with all their props and luggage. The young woman took the young stationmaster by the arm and went on a tour of inspection. He later said that he was so dazzled by her that he would have agreed to anything. She soon fixed upon a stationhouse room – the largest waiting room – and, with the help of a couple of porters, it was cleared and arranged to her order.

'Where does that door lead to,' she said, pointing to one in the wall.

'To the stationmaster's office,' came the reply.

'The very thing,' she said. "Door in flat" we'll call it. You won't mind us using it, will you?'

The young man began to explain about the strict stationmaster who was due back later that evening.

'We shall probably be done before he gets back; but if we shouldn't, introduce me to him directly. I think I shall be able to manage him,' said the young woman.

All the furniture of the room was arranged round this door as she required it, and the rest of the company filed in. To the young man's horror, Miss Totts – he had by this time discovered her name – had made considerable changes in the stationmaster's sanctum. His desk had been turned round, and his big washstand, which no one dared to touch in his absence, was being carried to the other end of the room by one of the porters, who certainly would not have dared to do it under normal circumstances, even if a director of the railway had commanded it.

Miss Totts then commanded all the station staff to be the audience. No one refused, so dazzled were they by her beauty and air of authority. She said: 'You shall see what no London audience, or any other audience, has seen yet – the principal act of our new comedy.'

And with that, the station – a main-line junction station at that – came to a complete standstill, as the staff and any passenger waiting for trains gathered to watch a play in the waiting room. The young assistant stationmaster later said it was the most enjoyable two hours of his life – yet curiously he was unable to remember the name of the play.

When at last the play was over, railway staff and passengers all burst into a thunder of applause. The whole of the platform staff had been watching the play, and, at the very moment the young man realised quite the disruption that had been caused to the normal running of the station, he spotted the stationmaster. 'I'm dead,' he thought.

The stationmaster, a look of fury on his face, went to the door of the waiting room, which he threw open, looking in upon the laughing, chattering crowd.

'What's the meaning o' this discreditable neglect,' he said, turning to the young man.

He was about to reply when Miss Totts appeared as if from nowhere.

'Are you the stationmaster?' she said, looking at the old gentleman with her unforgettable smile. 'Oh I'm so glad you've come,' and she held out her hand. 'I was so anxious to tell you how kind and considerate your deputy has been to us all, and so have all your men. I'm sure if all railway stations were as well managed as this is, it would be a pleasure to come to them, instead of the nuisance it generally is. Pray come in, for we have an additional favour to ask.'

It was impossible to resist her. The old man's face visibly softened as Miss Totts passed her hand through his arm. A few moments later she was pouring him out a glass of wine, and he was looking at her over the rim of the glass with an expression of fatherly benignity. They wanted to do the play over again, and they actually got the old gentleman to keep the engine and train waiting while they did it. The old Presbyterian stationmaster was like a happy child who would have shut down the whole network if Miss Totts had asked him to.

At last the play was over and the company had climbed aboard their train. As it ran out of the station, the railway staff set up a huge cheer, and the last thing anyone saw, according to the young stationmaster, was 'Miss Totts' sweet, pretty face looking at us out of the window as she waved her hand in farewell.'

But when the train had gone the young stationmaster knew he would have to face the wrath of the stationmaster and he would almost certainly be sacked. The old man walked straight up to him. 'She's a bonny lassie, Johnny,' he said. 'She's a bonnie lassie, and a young man might, perhaps, be forgiven his duty a point when she's aboot.'

SNATCHBURY

ENGLAND, 1879

Men have always been fascinated by steam trains. Even before they were consigned to the long oblivion of history, moves were afoot to keep at least some of them running on preserved lines. Women rarely become so passionate about steam, but dogs occasionally share their master's passions.

For several years there was, for example, a bright little English terrier that travelled regularly from King's Cross to Doncaster seated on the toolbox between the driver and the fireman. Hail, rain, or sunshine, the dog would be seen sticking to his post, while the engine dashed along at full speed, and the wind brushed out the little dog's coat till it looked as if it were made of bristles. Several other dogs are recorded as inveterate train travellers but few are able to match the fame of the near legendary Snatchbury.

Snatchbury was known as the prince of drivers' dogs, his adventures reported regularly in *The Times* and other newspapers. His story began when, out of the blue, he turned up one day at Euston, dodging about on the platform, evidently looking for a friend. Having chosen his platform the dog sat down and looked questioningly out along the track. A train came into the station right by the platform where the little dog sat waiting, and the driver, known as 'the Duke', from his aquiline nose, caught sight of the dog, and called him. The little rough-haired, small-headed lump of light-brown doggyness jumped on to the footplate, and scrambled up to the back of the tender. Twenty minutes later, off went the train, and with it went Snatchbury, as he came to be christened.

For ten years afterwards, by night and day, through fog and sunshine, Snatchbury stuck to the Duke, and, with his shaggy hair blown back so as to show his white teeth, hardly ever missed his engine. Every day he would come on duty and race down the engines in the shed till he found the right one, and if it had been moved he would leap and whine till it was pointed out to him.

One day he came too late. His favourite driver was just going out of the station. Snatchbury was distraught but he was also an observant dog. He waited till the next engine going the same way started, and then he jumped on that train and went to Rugby, where he changed engines to Bletchley, and there caught up with the Duke!

Snatchbury's intelligence was remarkable. He learned the signals, and could tell whether they were up or down, or red or green; and if a red light was shown ahead he would announce the fact with a warning bark. Even the fog-signals he came to know the meaning of, and he would bark to announce the dangerous ones! In fact, Snatchbury took an intelligent interest in all that he came across, and seemed never to forget what he saw. And he was a kind-hearted dog too. His face was often seen by passengers and railway workers alike on the engine at Euston, leaning over and looking along the train; and if he noticed a strange dog being put into the brake van by the guard, he would jump down and run in to the new arrival to have a quick sniff and a tail-wagging session before returning to his place at the engine!

Then one terrible night a signalman at Harrow made a mistake, and showed the line as being all clear when a goods train was in the way. On came the Duke in obedience to the signal full speed into the trucks he could not see. He was killed instantly. Snatchbury was hurled off with him, but was unhurt. The dog's grief was heartbreaking. At the funeral the dog walked beside the coffin. Back at the driver's common room, the Duke's boots were placed by the fire, as though ready for him when he came back. And with his nose between his paws poor Snatchbury waited there for the master he was never again to see. After a time Snatchbury recovered somewhat and took to another driver; but it did not last long. When he died some years later Snatchbury was taken to the taxidermist, stuffed and put into a glass case. His current whereabouts are unknown.

AMIABLE LUNATIC

FRANCE, 1880

To travel with a lunatic is not an agreeable experience, but travel long enough and far enough by train and you will certainly encounter the mad, the bad and sometimes the dangerous to know. An English businessman who travelled to the South of France and back towards the end of the nineteenth century recorded his meeting with what he described as an amiable lunatic; the sort of person who, though not quite dangerous, is vaguely alarming and seems to delight in doing things that are unnerving, to say the least.

Having reached Marseilles and conducted his business the Englishman toured the city for a few days. In an account of his adventure written towards the end of his life, and published anonymously, he remembered the pleasure of Marseilles:

> It is such a wonderfully bright, busy, bustling place. There is a Moorish look about the old Southern town, and the people one sees walking about the dusty streets are of the most polyglot description. The turban and the fez are quite common, and Oriental and European languages are spoken almost indiscriminately. My friends were kind, the weather was superb, and altogether I had a delightful time.

Monday was the day set for his departure, but he spent much of it wandering the city on foot to the extent that by the time he arrived at the station he was dog-tired and looking forward to a good sleep in his compartment on the way back. But it was not

176

to be. He reached the St Charles station just in time for the rapide train to Paris.

The Englishman takes up the story of what happened next:

The spick-and-span conductor of the sleeping car – for the International Sleeping Car Company had one of their luxurious vehicles on the train – handed me a telegram from a French friend who was going to join the train at Dijon at about 4 o'clock the next morning. He remarked, at the same time, that it looked as if I were to have the compartment – with berths for four – all to myself that night.

Throwing my weary body on the seat, I waited for the train to set off. Just then I heard voices carrying on an animated discussion in the corridor, and an instant later two ladies and an old gentleman burst into the compartment. For a moment I thought our conductor, a Dutchman, was about to plant the three of them on me, in the coup for the night, which would have been awkward for me – modesty and the rules of social intercourse would have forced me, despite my exhausted state, immediately to move to another compartment.

However, the two ladies – and they were both young and pretty – put the old gentleman into a nice, cool alpaca coat and left him. After having quitted the car, they stood on the platform as the train moved out of the station. They blew kisses to the old man till we were out of sight.

It was at this point that the Englishman noticed the old man putting a large red handkerchief to his face. He then heaved three massive sighs into its voluminous folds and a pigeon appeared as if from nowhere from the folds. 'There you are you little rogue!' he said.

The Englishman couldn't believe his eyes, but having regained his composure simply assumed that this was a practising magician. In the next moment the Dutchman – for that is what he seemed to be judging by his accent – had opened the window of the train, shouted 'Now go home you bugger!' and thrown the bird into the slipstream. The magician, if that is indeed what he was, then looked across at the Englishman with a radiant smile on his face.

'Good evening, Monsieur,' he said. 'It's rather warm tonight is it not?'

'Yes, sir, very warm indeed,' replied the Englishman.

Seeing that he was ready for a long conversation, the Englishman, who desperately wanted to sleep, tried to cut him short by saying, 'Excuse me, sir; I am an Englishman, and do not speak French very fluently. Besides, I have been walking about all day and am tired.'

But the old man took absolutely no notice and began paying the Englishman extravagant compliments about the excellence of his French.

'You are an Englishman, and I am Flemish; we both speak French, and are compelled to remain here for the next fifteen or sixteen hours. Why, then, we must have a good talk?' The Englishman's heart sank – without being rude this was going to be a very difficult situation to escape

But then conversation was not, as it turned out, quite what the old man had in mind. He began a long rambling account of his own life.

'You must not think I have been travelling on a journey of pleasure,' he said. 'For I did not leave Brussels until Saturday, reaching Marseilles last night (Sunday); and here I am on my way back again.' Then, leaning over the table, he said in a whisper, while dramatically striking his forehead two heavy smacks with the palm of his fat hand, 'My wife's sister is ill. Do you see?'

'Yes,' said the Englishman to himself, 'I do see; she's clearly barking mad and it occurs to me that you are ill in the same way too.'

But needing no encouragement the old man continued as before.

'Those two young ladies are my nieces. They are the daughters of a bank manager who plans to vanish and I've been called in – though I am by profession a baker – to find him once he's gone.'

At this point the old man pulled out his purse and displayed a huge number of bright golden coins. 'What do you think of these?' he asked, as he extended his gloved hand. In an instant, the gold had vanished to be replaced by a handful of gaudy-looking jewellery. He showed the Englishman numerous pieces of the most tawdry jewellery.

'A present for my wife,' said the old man, 'Well, I mean I will give them to my wife when I find her and marry her.'

By this time the Englishman was half alarmed and half amused, but he felt too tired to indulge any view of the old man for long such was his desperation for sleep.

'What if he attacks me?' thought the Englishman, who considered asking the conductor to move him to another compartment. But the innate English desire not to cause offence kept him in his seat. The old man continued to chatter about any and every thing, speaking ever more quickly with extravagant gestures and wildly flailing arms, while the Englishman prayed that he might shut up even if only for five minutes so he could get some sleep.

But the old man was enjoying himself now. 'Have you seen the inside of my coat?' he asked. Hardly bothering to wait for an answer, he whisked off his coat to reveal an extraordinary satin lining decorated with strange hieroglyphs and bizarre markings.

'I believe this explains the inner secrets of the heavens and the secret of our world,' said the old man. 'If you know how to read it – and I don't – it will also give you all of Europe's railway timetables including details of which trains will be delayed.' He winked at the Englishman and pulled out a horribly messy packet of sandwiches.

'Sea slug,' he said with a knowing look while tapping the side of his nose. 'Sea slug explains my great age and youthful appearance. I won't tell you when I was born lest you find me suspicious.'

He then began to tap dance and swirl about the carriage shouting incomprehensible things about his cape and the contents of his pockets. But, after ten minutes of this, exhaustion clearly got the better of him and he flopped down into the seat next to the Englishman. He then became enormously concerned about the Englishman's welfare and offered to buy him wine, brandy, a cigar, a box of handkerchiefs, a rifle and two cummerbunds. The list seemed to go on forever and grew ever more bizarre.

The train stopped at Avignon, and the Englishman stood in the corridor looking out on to the platform, viewing the movements of a number of passengers and the usual incidents of station life, so familiar and yet so strange. With an inward groan he then heard the voice of his travelling companion. Stepping back into his compartment, the Englishman saw that the old man now had a large clasp knife in one hand and in the other hand a long square bar of ordinary washing soap.

'You would like some cheese?' he said indicating to both knife and soap and in a moment a piece of the soap was in his mouth, and a moment later he was spitting and spluttering on the floor of the car.

'Ah Monsieur,' he said with tears in his eyes, 'I love it but it is so strong I'm sure it is bad for me.'

By now the Englishman was thoroughly alarmed but at the same time he felt powerless to do anything about his situation. Still he had not been able to sleep and he was so tired that he felt on the verge of hallucinating.

About then the conductor came in to the compartment and explained that a one-legged man had asked if the Englishman would mind having the upper bunk in order that the one legged man should not have to climb to a difficult height.

The Englishman immediately realised, and with huge relief, that this was his chance to escape the attention of the old man. He agreed to move up to the upper bunk and immediately did so, refusing to come down again despite the pleas of the old man.

When he realised that his companion was not going to continue their conversation the old man announced in a loud voice that his grandfather, the sultan, never went to bed before three in the morning and he intended to continue the family tradition. Thus, on the few occasions when the Englishman dared peep over the edge of his bunk, he saw the old man sitting on the floor, cross-legged and smoking an extremely long pipe.

The train stopped at Valence, and it was nearly midnight. It seemed ages since dinnertime, and the Englishman was hungry. Through the window he could see young men selling rolls, butter and jams from trays but how on earth could he go out and buy these things when the madman was still sitting on the floor?

The answer came in an instant when the Englishman looked once again over the edge of his bed. Below, where the old man had been, there was nothing. A second later the door of the compartment opened and the old man appeared with rolls, butter and coffee for the Englishman, the one-legged man and himself. As he tucked into this most welcome food the Englishman almost felt some affection for the man who had driven him to the edge of distraction.

Another man had now entered their compartment and the old man was entertaining *him* with bizarre tales and dances, odd snatches of song and poetry. At one stage he also pulled up the leg of his trousers to show the newcomer a wound he claimed he'd received during the Crimean War. At last, at 3 o'clock in the morning, the old man agreed to go to sleep.

In the morning the old man was up first and he was talking to the Englishman even before the Englishman was fully awake.

'We are near Brussels,' he said. 'You must accompany me on a grand tour in my private coach.'

'No, thank you, Monsieur,' said the Englishman.

'But I'll pay, I'll pay!' came the reply.

The Englishman explained that he was meeting a friend and then going straight on to England. The old man was devastated and began to weep. The Englishman, overcome with embarrassment, shook his hand. When last he looked back along the platform the old man had turned his extraordinary coat inside out and was sitting on a bench playing a small set of bagpipes of a type the Englishman had never seen before.

LOVE ON THE TRAIN

FRANCE, 1880

He might have been Turkish or Greek or from North Africa. Certainly he had at least three, possibly four places of birth according to his own account, which varied according to time and circumstance. No one quite knew when he was born but Zacharie Zacharoff (who went also under a number of pseudonyms) was certainly born into poverty, probably in Constantinople in the 1840s or 1850s. He was, by all accounts, born of doubtful parentage and raised in great poverty in the dusty streets of that crumbling city. Yet half a century later he had been awarded one of France's highest honours, the Legion d'Honneur – after a life of extraordinary intrigue. But the pivotal point of his life was, without question, an extraordinary journey on the *Orient Express*, that symbol of pre-Great War luxury that died slowly only with the coming of luxury passenger flying.

Zacharie spent his life living off his wits – that much is known for sure. After his earliest days in Constantinople, where he may have worked as a waiter, he vanished until the 1860s when he emerged suddenly with a wife and another name – Manel Sohar. In the 1870s he began working for an uncle's general merchant business. He then vanished again before reappearing in England, where he somehow developed a connection with an arms firm and began selling their weapons to various governments in Central and Eastern Europe.

Whenever he travelled across Europe, he took the *Orient Express* and each time he did so, he contacted an Albanian pimp who supplied him with a redhead – it had to be a redhead – for the duration of the journey. He became very rich and spent more and more time on the *Orient Express*, travelling ever more widely and selling increasing number of weapons. Soon the railway staff grew so used to him that they bowed when he arrived at the platform and no official at any border crossing would dare to ask to see his passport. He was treated as only the members of European royal families were treated.

Only once was he kept waiting and that was at the beginning of what was to prove a most extraordinary journey. He was held for a few moments while waiting to board the *Orient Express* while a young Spanish couple were allowed through. They were Don Francisco y Bourbon, a cousin of the Spanish King Alphonso XII, and his young bride, who were setting off for their honeymoon. Zacharie was astonished at how unhappy they looked, but soon they had vanished into the luxurious carriage, which was reserved for them, and he thought no more of it.

Late that night, as the train hurtled across the dark landscape, Zacharoff heard loud and terrifying screaming. A few moments later, he opened the door of his compartment and discovered a torn, bleeding and half-dressed young and very beautiful woman, whom he instantly recognised as the young Spanish bride he'd earlier seen boarding the train. She looked straight into his eyes and said almost in a whisper 'Save me! He will kill me!'

Then Zacharoff noticed that a short way along the corridor one of his servants was wrestling a fearsome-looking dagger from the hand of a young man who lunged and kicked like someone out of his mind. Zacharoff invited the girl into his compartment, shut the door and made her comfortable. It is said that by the time the train reached Vienna, some three hours later, Zacharoff was in love. It was a love that was to supersede all previous loves – including redheads – and it lasted till the end of Zacharoff's life.

At Vienna, the young bridegroom was bundled away by a group of officials and taken to an asylum. The young woman went with them and Zacharoff may have thought that was the last he would see of her. But somehow, after the extraordinary events on the train, Zacharoff and the young woman – whom he knew as Doña Maria –

managed to correspond with each other and Zacharoff soon discovered that the young woman's mad husband had been escorted back to Spain.

Soon Maria became an outcast – nothing could be the fault of the Spanish royal family, so the young man's madness was blamed on the cruelty of the woman who had abandoned him. She was sent into exile and joined Zacharoff permanently on his long journeys across Europe and always on the train on which they'd first met.

As the years passed they had three children, all daughters, and Zacharoff grew ever richer. Eventually he was employed as the arms manufacturer Vicker's top man in Europe. By 1922 Don Francisco – the mad bridegroom – was still in an asylum but he was 62 and in ill health. Zacharoff was in his seventies and his name was a legend.

Zacharoff astonished the world in 1923 by buying the Monte Carlo casino for the then-unheard-of sum of a million pounds. At last, in 1924, Don Francisco died, after a lifetime's confinement in an asylum. Then, after almost forty years to the day after they had met on the train, Zacharoff and Doña Maria were married. Two years later she was dead. After her death Zacharoff never again travelled on the *Orient Express*. He was fabulously wealthy but gradually became a recluse before dying at last in 1936.

The evening following his death, in accordance with the strict instructions left in his will, two of Zacharoff's servants took the *Orient Express* from Paris towards Salzburg. At 2.30am precisely – the exact time Zacharoff had first met Doña Maria – one of the two took a photograph of Doña Maria and her three daughters from his pocket, tore them into pieces and scattered them out through the window of the speeding train into the cold night air.

PLATFORM DOG

ENGLAND, 1880

There are many stories concerning dogs travelling alone by train. Several dogs are known to have crossed the northern wastes of Russia on the trans-Siberian railway unaccompanied and, on occasion, dogs have accidentally hopped on to trains that have taken them hundreds of miles from home.

At Reading at the end of the nineteenth century there was even a platform dog that ran around the station with a special leather collection box tied to its back collecting money for charity. It took regular trips to London, presumably hoping to raise even more cash for good causes. It was so popular that when it died it was stuffed and put in a big glass case on the platform and it was still there well into the 1970s.

But perhaps the most extraordinary animal traveller of all was a dog that with an almost human instinct always seemed to know where he wanted to go and how to get there. He was known as Railway Jack, and belonging to a former stationmaster at Lewes who, in the early 1880s, was a frequent traveller on the trains between that station and London.

Railway's Jack's knowledge of the timetable was vast. He appeared to know all the trains up and down and travelled, so far as anyone could make out, for the pure love of it. He would often get out of the train at intermediate stations for a saunter in the countryside or to greet the rustic railway staff, but never missed the last train home.

A remarkable fact about Jack was that he was never known to take the wrong train. Once, when placed by a porter in the guard's van of a train that was not going to his destination, he appeared to sense in some extraordinary way that matters were not right. So he jumped out and returned to the platform waiting room until his train to Lewes arrived.

Jack travelled all over the South-East for years visiting all the major towns and many tiny villages where there were stations. Passengers were always delighted to see him; he was adored by schoolchildren and universally missed when at the age of about eighteen he died in his sleep.

DANGEROUS PRACTICES

AMERICA, 1881

An Englishman visiting America was astonished at the dangerous way in which some American railways were run. On one journey he heard the sound of feet running on the roof above his head while the train roared along at more than fifty miles per hour. On each occasion, before the train entered a tunnel, the Englishman noticed a loud thump on the roof overhead.

He discovered later that the practice on American trains was to fit brake screw handles to the roofs of the carriages. This meant that the brakeman had to run along the top of the vehicles, applying the brakes when necessary. This was a terrifying business in rough weather, and especially so where there were tunnels. As a protective warning, overhanging gantries with hanging whipcord pellets were provided not far from the tunnels, so that the men on the roofs were hit by the pellets and knew it was time to throw themselves flat or be killed!

LOST TRAINS

ENGLAND, 1881

On the Settle and Carlisle railway, in 1881, every device for getting through a huge snow drift was tried in vain when the train became snowed up completely. Only the top of the engine funnel appeared above the white waste and a passing navvy walking high up on the packed snow is reported to have used the six inches of the funnel still visible as a spittoon!

Apart from the buried train, the signs that this was an extraordinarily bad storm were everywhere: stations were buried, passengers died of hypothermia and telegraph wires were so covered with ice and snow that, in places, they were as thick as a man's arm.

Elsewhere, the drifts in Cumberland were more than forty feet deep, and out of them were dug ten cold locomotives that had been buried for weeks. The same storm cost the Great Western £56,000, much of that the cost of having to excavate over a hundred miles of snow from three to ten feet thick, in which were buried 51 passenger trains and thirteen goods trains.

During the same storm, a North-Eastern engine went northwards out of Gateshead, and began work by driving through a drift a mile and a half long and 14 feet high, finally reaching a cutting where the snow had solidified into so compact a mass that the engine stuck fast. From the Monday morning to the following Saturday night, none of the men at work to clear the tracks were ever able to go home. They slept in their clothes in a makeshift hut. For 38 hours they were without water, except that obtained by melting the snow. It was a miracle no one died.

PONY RIDES

ENGLAND, 1882

The Eastern Counties Railway service was famous for its delays and lack of punctuality. The anecdote that best summed this up concerned a woman and her son. The boy was clearly well beyond the age at which he was entitled to a half fare so there was a slight disagreement between the woman and station staff when she reached the end of her journey.

The ticket inspector said: 'This child is too old for a half fare.'

The woman replied: 'He may be now but he wasn't when we bought the ticket!'

But if the Eastern Counties railways were plagued by bad timekeeping they were also occasionally plagued by eccentric travellers. On one journey the guard was summoned by a passenger who claimed she could hear heavy scuffling and knocking sounds from the compartment next to hers. The noises had been intermittent but occasionally violent. She explained that she'd tried to open the door of the compartment to check that all was well but it seemed to be locked. She'd also noticed that the blinds were pulled down so there was no way to check that the occupants had not suffered, as she put it, 'some dreadful calamity'.

The guard suspected that the woman was actually just being nosy and was happy to use any excuse to find out what was going on in the darkened compartment but he felt he had to at least humour her. He'd just begun to explain that some travellers liked to sleep or were simply concerned not to be disturbed when he heard a violent thud. In fact, it was so violent it almost seemed that the compartment might burst.

189

The guard knocked cautiously on the compartment door. There was no reply. He knocked again and said: 'Good morning. This is the guard. Are you all right?' Still no reply. Then another thud followed by loud shufflings. The guard told the woman still standing by his side that he would summon help. He returned with the ticket collector and they managed to force the door. Inside they found a middle-aged and very portly man asleep in a corner seat by the window. Filling the rest of the compartment between the two rows of seats that faced each other was a small but very nervous-looking pony.

In the instant they realised what it was, the pony kicked out its back legs and narrowly missed the guard. The door jamb splintered under the impact of the pony's iron-shod hooves and the fat man woke up. Rather than apologise for the outrage of putting a pony on the train in this way the man argued that his sleep had been interrupted by the guard and ticket collector. He simply would not accept that he had done anything wrong. When he and his pony were ejected at the next station he swore the company would be hearing from his solicitors. In fact, he was never heard of again.

How he managed to get the pony on to the train in the first place without anyone noticing remains a complete mystery.

DIVER SAVES THE RAIL TUNNEL

ENGLAND, 1884

Railway journeys from England to Wales would have been far more difficult in Victorian times but for the extraordinary pioneering work of the early engineers who built the Severn Tunnel. Work on the tunnel, through very difficult ground, had been continuing for some time and drainage pumps had been carefully fitted along the length of the existing tunnel to keep the railway tracks dry. The track had been laid to allow men and equipment to be moved easily to and from the front of the tunnel, where the cutting was taking place. It was extremely dangerous work at a time when the science of tunnelling was still at best pretty rudimentary.

A flood door – like a bulkhead in a ship – had been provided in the tunnel, so that, in the case of a sudden and a massive influx of water, the door could be quickly shut by the men as they ran for their lives. It was hoped that the door would hold back the water at least long enough for the men to escape.

The main tunnel had also been provided with ladders that reached up into a higher (and theoretically drier) tunnel. The engineers knew they were working close to what was known as the Great Spring, but they thought their calculations were precise enough to keep them clear of it. They were wrong. Suddenly the Great Spring was broken into and a vast flood, estimated at 27,000 gallons per minute, smashed its way into the tunnels, sweeping engineering trains, wagons and men out of its way like so much matchwood.

In the hurried scramble to get the survivors out, the workmen forgot to close the flood door. The flooding was on such a vast scale that the pumps were overpowered, and the main tunnel, the higher tunnel and all the shafts were filled to the level of the water in the Severn.

For the time being the tunnel works were completely lost – months of hard work wasted. Just a few feet at the top of the shaft were left showing. Before anything else could be done the flood door – still open but now hundreds of yards down below the black debris-filled water – had to be closed. The question was, how on earth could it be done? Even today such a task would be extremely difficult but it could at least be attempted without risk to life by sending down an unmanned probe or mini-submarine of some kind. In Victorian times the only option was a diver. Someone had to be found to make such a dangerous dive.

Diving equipment was crude and primitive, and underwater lighting equipment non-existent. Those who gathered to discuss the crisis knew that any attempt would have only a fifty per cent chance of success at best. The chances of failure – and inevitable death for the diver – were just too high. And, even if they could get a volunteer, the distance involved was too great for any diver to descend, dragging his air-tube and life-line with him.

But the railway tunnel engineers were not about to give up. They made enquiries and discovered that Britain's most experienced and highly paid diver had on one or two occasions attempted dives that should have led to his certain death. On each occasion he had survived simply, it was said, because he never lost his head, however difficult the circumstances. His name was Lambert and it cost the railway company a fortune to engage his services.

For superstitious reasons, and to ensure that it had warmed up before a dive (thus reducing the risk of condensation), Lambert always wore his diving mask on the journey to a particular job. And thus it was that on a summer's day early in the staid and respectable middle decades of Victoria's reign, a first-class carriage leaving the London terminus contained a man in a very smart suit but wearing a large ungainly diver's helmet. Perhaps it is not surprising that he had the carriage to himself on that extraordinary journey.

As soon as he arrived at the flooded entrance to the tunnel he was helped into the rest of his equipment and he quickly disappeared into the murky waters. In the days leading up to his dive, Lambert had studied intently every available drawing of the tunnels, the position at which the water was entering them and the exact location of the flood door.

He later described his nightmare journey through the flooded water. The tunnel was almost completely blocked with floating timber, trucks and tubs, rails and heaps of bricks. Lambert had to go down a secondary shaft, then walk in absolute darkness down to the main tunnel, which was no easy matter to find, and which he had then to descend. Finally, he had to walk along what was known as the drainage heading, a total distance of 400 yards, in order to reach the door.

Only those who've done some diving, perhaps in murky English seas, will have any idea of what Lambert's journey through the flooded tunnels must have been like. It would have been pitch dark and with no landmarks or sense of direction or orientation, the journey would have created a feeling of intense panic in all but the most resilient. Lambert must have known too that he was entirely on his own and that if something went wrong he would be lost forever – there was no hope of rescue.

He went down for an hour, returned, and had failed. He was induced to make a second attempt, the pumps being worked to the utmost capacity during his absence, but no lowering of the water was observable. He was away so long that the gathering railway officials were convinced he had joined the dozens of other dead men still trapped beneath the murky waters. Then, just when all hope had gone, suddenly the water in the shaft began and continued to fall, showing that Lambert – against all the odds – had succeeded, and had shut the door and thus excluded the waters from the Great Spring.

This act saved the tunnel but, more importantly, it showed that the railway builders were able to surmount the greatest difficulties and dangers. The Severn Tunnel became a monument not only to the skill of the tunnelling and railway engineers, but also to the indomitable courage of Lambert the diver – who emerged from his labours entirely unscathed.

FAST WORKER

AMERICA, 1884

America is and has always been seen as a rather fast country. American cars, trains and aeroplanes are always either faster or certainly ultimately bigger than anyone else's.

Occasionally the American enthusiasm for speed – for, if you like, cutting to the chase – spills over into areas of personal morality and one of the most extraordinary incidents of this kind was reported in the *Cincinnati Commercial* newspaper in 1884.

The incident occurred on the Little Miami Railway. A woman of about forty was travelling to Cincinnati on the 8.45am express. The train was crowded, so when a man of about the same age climbed aboard halfway through the journey he had difficulty finding a seat. Eventually, having walked the length of the train, he found a seat by the woman and began to talk to her.

By the time the train arrived at its destination an hour later the man had proposed and the woman had accepted, although she later said she thought it was all just a bit of a joke. At the station they parted, the woman to a hotel, the man to get a marriage licence.

When he appeared at her hotel, licence in hand, she was astonished. Her astonishment had nothing to do with the fact that his arrival was proof positive that he'd really meant what he said on the train – no, she was astonished that it had taken him so long to get the licence and get back to her!

They were married for forty years and discovered soon after their wedding day that they had been to the same first school and were even distantly related.

194

WHITE ELEPHANT

ENGLAND, 1884

When the great showman P T Barnham – the Prince of Humbugs as he later became known – brought his extraordinary circus-cum-menagerie from America to England in 1884 it was billed as the wonder of the age. But when the train arrived in London, carrying his celebrated white elephant from Rangoon, there was almost a riot. People had begun crowding round the station hours before the specially adapted train arrived. And of course the levels of excitement rose as the time went by and the crowds grew bigger. Then the train came slowly into the station, the specially adapted carriage was opened and a very ordinary-looking Indian elephant walked cautiously down the ramp on to the platform. The crowds went wild, but not with excitement and wonder: with outrage. As the riot took hold – bottles and bricks were thrown, top hats were ground into the dust – it took several hundred police more than an hour to restore order. Barnham was unperturbed by the fuss and his menagerie continued its tour to sell-out audiences.

Barnham had been born into rural poverty in Bethel, Connecticut in 1810. He'd started on the road to fame and fortune by buying and exhibiting a woman he claimed was 170 years old. She was actually about seventy – a fact that somehow or other became clear when she died. Barnham was disgraced. Bloody but unbowed he then bought a dwarf – the celebrated Tom Thumb – and a museum of freaks and oddities and continued to tour America, drawing huge crowds with boasts about the show that were not always borne out by the show itself. Barnham was the first great spin doctor. He believed that people saw what you told them they were going to see, provided you were truly convincing. He was the first to use sensational forms of publicity to popularise his circus. In partnership with James A Bailey, he made the American circus a popular and gigantic spectacle, the so-called Greatest Show on Earth.

At the height of his success he had a train specially built so that his animals could all get in at one end and walk through all the carriages to get to their allotted places. Apart from his circus and his extraordinary train, Barnham is perhaps best known for coining the phrase: 'There's a sucker born every minute.' He died in 1891.

REFUND FOR THE DEAD

GERMANY, 1885

A miserly interest in money is not an attractive quality. Railway travellers are not afflicted especially with a grasping love of money but, in at least one recorded instance, the family of a traveller took thrift to absurd – and embarrassing – lengths. It began when the head of the family, an elderly but apparently healthy individual, bought his ticket and then reached platform six at Dresden station.

He walked towards his train, keeled over without any warning and was dead by the time two porters had reached him to try to help.

During the days that followed, the dead man's family tried to claim a refund on his ticket. Initially the request for the refund was just a detail in the general business of sorting out the dead man's affairs but, as time passed, it became an obsession and far more was spent on legal wrangling than could every have been justified by the cost of the ticket itself. The family argued in court that their dead relative had not even stepped aboard the train and was therefore entitled to a refund. Why the railway company decided to dig their heels in over this no one will ever know, but they did and they successfully counter-argued in front of one of Germany's most famous judges that the dead man was obliged at the very least to pay for a platform ticket, since he had reached the platform and had had the audacity to die right there on the railway company's property.

On the last day of the court case the judge decided that the dead man's family was entitled to a refund, less the cost – precisely one penny – of a platform ticket. The costs of the case were undisclosed but must have run into thousands of marks.

COWBOYS

AMERICA, 1886

The relative lawlessness of much of nineteenth-century rural America meant that country railroad conductors (or guards, as they would be known in the UK) were selected as much for brawn and muscle as for mental and moral qualifications. American trains had to travel difficult, and often dangerous terrain and events that might seem extraordinary in Europe were almost everyday occurrences in the States. Tragedies of revenge were often acted out on the train and, as the following story reveals, with dreadful consequences.

A certain conductor, a six-foot-six ex-boxer, was well known to all the cowboys and patrons of his particular route for his amiability, courage and enormous strength. One day he was sitting chatting to a newspaperman he knew well. They were in the rear of the carriage and, during a lull in the conversation, the conductor pointed to the only other passengers that the car contained, namely a cowboy, his wife and baby, and said, 'That's Davy Muller. He has a ranch 25 miles west of Valentine.' When the train arrived at the next station, a big, rough-looking man got on and sat down a few seats ahead of the conductor and his friend, but seven or eight seats behind the cowboy and his family.

The conductor took the new passenger's fare, came back and whispered to his friend: 'You will see trouble presently. I will explain later; meantime pretend to be asleep and I will do the same.' After about half an hour, the big man who'd climbed aboard at the last station roused himself, looked cautiously around and, seeing the conductor and his companion apparently asleep, crept carefully on

198

tiptoe with a huge knife in his hand towards the cowboy, who was dandling his baby on his knee, unconscious of any danger.

The conductor saw what was about to happen and crept after the man in absolute silence. When the man with the knife reached the cowboy he shouted: 'Now I've got you, you bastard' and raised his knife to strike. The cowboy dropped the baby on to the floor as the knife descended, but it never reached its destination, for the conductor grasped the man by the arm and wrestled him to the floor. The knife skittered across the floor of the railway carriage, and the newspaperman picked it up. The would-be murderer was hustled into the smoking carriage. At the next station the cowboy jumped from the train and ran to the telegraph office from which he sent a message to his friends in Valentine asking them to meet him at the station, armed.

The telegraph operator who had sent the message wired the conductor on the train to let him know that even more trouble would be waiting if the would-be assassin was still on the train when it reached Valentine. To avoid this, the conductor decided to drop the man off well before the station.

After arranging this checkmate, the conductor returned to his bemused friend the newspaperman, to explain what was going on. The two men, it seemed, were brothers-in-law, having married sisters. The would-be murderer was a government inspector of cattle, who lived two miles south of Valentine; when sober, he was intelligent, cultivated and well behaved, but in his cups he was a monster. At such times he abused his wife, and the brother-in-law having defended her had caused the quarrel.

The two men had already fought a duel in which the cattle inspector received a wound, which had laid him up for several weeks. 'I'll try to get him to drop off the train one station this side of Valentine,' said the conductor. But the cattle inspector refused to do this; he didn't care who was waiting for him at Valentine.

'All right,' said the conductor, 'but I shall slow up a mile this side of Valentine and you will jump off or I will throw you off.' The inspector knew the conductor would do as he said, and so he jumped off. Sure enough, when the train arrived at Valentine, a dozen wild-looking cowboys leaped aboard, brandishing knives and guns, running along the carriages and shouting 'Where is he? Show us the god-damned son of a coyote.'

Failing to get their man, the wild men took the cowboy and his family under their wing and rode off, firing their guns, and vowing to get the inspector if ever he showed up again in that region. The next morning, when passing down to the land office, the newspaperman saw seven ponies hitched outside a café. Inside were seven wild-looking men, their rifles beside them, taking breakfast. The newspaper man recognised all of them from the bunch of cowboys who'd boarded the train the previous day. One among them was the cowboy from the train. As the railwaymen passed, the men came out, mounted their ponies and rode off toward the cattle inspector's cabin.

'What's up?' said the newspaperman to a lean, long-haired Native American who stood propping up a telegraph pole outside the town hotel. The reply was not helpful: 'Now look here,' said the man, 'I've got troubles enough of my own, an' if you think I'm going to be drawn into other folks' you've missed the trail and I'm travellin' through the wilderness.'

Without telling his wife that trouble was in the air, the cattle inspector had risen early that morning and set off on horseback in search of a stray cow that had been missing for several days. He went unarmed, except for a revolver stuck in his belt. He was about a mile north of his house when the horsemen spotted him. An extraordinary race ensued, with the cattle inspector riding for his life, while the others rode for revenge.

By some strange process of telepathy the whole town seemed at once aware of what was going on, and manned every vantage point from which a view of the race might be had. A glance showed the inspector that his enemies would cut him off before he could regain his house and he turned and spurred for the river, where there was cover.

Hardly believing what was happening, the newspaperman watched them sweep over the plain, the pursued holding his own gamely, but at last they disappeared into the trees and thick cover and in an instant the citizens of Valentine carried on as if nothing untoward had happened. No one attempted to go to the aid of the inspector; they simply awaited developments. At about one o'clock that afternoon the cowboy and his six friends rode slowly into the town, their horses exhausted; no questions were asked, but an hour or two later friends of the inspector rode out to the river bank and found his dead body riddled with bullets and lying under a tree, his empty revolver still clutched in his stiffened fingers. The next day, an inquest was held and on the jury sat the seven men who had killed him; needless to say the verdict was, 'Shot by parties unknown.'

When the railway conductor and his friend the newspaperman went to see the widow of the dead man a few days later she greeted them with a composed air. They offered to help in any way they could. She said there would be no need – the people who were responsible for her husband's death would see that she wanted for nothing.

GENIUS OF THE IRISH

IRELAND, 1888

The Irish are passionate about horses and horse racing and when a big meet is on, sporting enthusiasts will do almost anything to avoid missing the big day.

Trains from Dublin to the Curragh were always packed on race day but on this particular day, 18 May, the packed train was pulling out of Dublin station when three young lads tore along the platform and jumped aboard. They'd arrived too late at the station to buy their tickets but knew that if they missed this train they'd miss the best of the day's sport. Once aboard they had a big problem. When the ticket collector appeared they would have some explaining to do – they had no tickets and would at the very least have to pay an excess fare and might even be fined.

'What on earth shall we do?' said one. 'We'll be prosecuted!'

'Nonsense,' said his friend with a knowing wink. 'We'll be fine.' Quite why he was confident he would not say, but, convinced of their friend's ability to get them out of a jam, they settled down to enjoy the journey.

When they reached the first station at which their tickets were almost certain to be examined the young man who'd been so sure they would be all right leapt out of his seat and ran out of the door of the compartment without a word. A few minutes later he dashed breathless back into the carriage but with three tickets held aloft.

'Where on earth did you get those?' said one of his friends.

'I went along till I found a carriage with some Englishmen in it – they had to be English for the Irish would be too cute to fall for it – and I just said "Tickets please!" and they handed them over without a murmur!'

STICKY TRACKS

AMERICA, 1888

In the eastern states of America, as was afterward true in the west, when the railroad expanded into those remote regions, it was often hard for those who lived in remote country districts to get trains to stop at their stations, and to secure other privileges upon which the growth of their settlements depended. In 1817, a little group of people had settled about a mile out of Medford, some six miles from Boston. They paid a visit to the offices of the superintendent of the railroad one day, with a request that he should stop the train at their admittedly tiny settlement. They argued that, once the train began to stop, the hamlet would grow first into a village, then a town and – who knows – maybe eventually a city.

The superintendent refused, point blank, simply because he believed he would lose money if he agreed to the plan. But the people of Medford refused to give up and persisted in their demands. When he remained firm in his refusal, they went away declaring they would make him stop the train whether he wanted to or not.

The superintendent took no notice of threats like this – he received them pretty regularly and often from individuals who took it as a personal affront that he would not agree to stop the train regularly at their individual farm houses!

There was a steep incline just outside Medford and a few days after the superintendent's meeting with the villagers the express train driver found that as he reached the incline his wheels began to slip. Within seconds, the train had come to a full stop and it stopped right by a group of Medford villagers.

They jumped aboard while the train driver got out to investigate the cause of the delay. He couldn't believe his eyes! The track for nearly a quarter of a mile up the incline had been smeared with – of all things – molasses.

The driver had to back his train up till he could get sufficient momentum to carry him over the hill. In the face of such persistence, there was no use in trying to run past Medford – the good citizens of that tiny hamlet got the regular stops they'd always wanted.

ON LEAVING THE RAILWAY

ENGLAND, 1889

Every railwayman engaged in the movement of trains – and that included guards, drivers, firemen, signalmen and stationmasters – was once supplied not only with the railway company's book of rules and regulations, itself a great tombstone of a book, but also with an even more hefty volume called *The Appendix to the Book of Rules and Regulations*, or more familiarly *The Appendix*.

The latter was the guards' and signalmen's bible, and applicants for both these positions had to know pretty much all its many provisions, which outline the course of action to be taken in a railway emergency. These books, together with uniform, clothing, hand lamp and other equipment supplied by the company, had to be returned when a railwayman left his job. But of course many men who left the various railway companies were rather keen – if they could get away with it – on not returning their equipment and that in turn led to all sorts of disputes and threats of litigation.

One anonymous clerk in the Great Western Railway stores at Swindon recorded a most amusing exchange when a company official wrote to an ex-railwayman asking for the return of the company's equipment. Bit by bit they got it back – everything, that is, except the former railwayman's copy of *The Appendix to the Book of Rules and Regulations*.

A solicitor's letter was sent out to the man asking him to send in his *Appendix* forthwith. Whether he wilfully misconstrued the request is not clear, but he replied: 'I've given up my job and sent in my uniform. I don't mind being unemployed so much, nor being unclothed, but I'm hanged if I'm going into hospital to be operated on!'

MOURNED BY ALL

SCOTLAND, 1890

When Jock the Perth railway dog died, he was mourned in the United States, in Russia and on both sides of the English Channel.

No one could quite remember when Jock first appeared, though it was generally agreed to be about 1890, when he was still a puppy. From the first, he was attracted to the footplate rather than the carriages, but as the years went by and his tastes matured he did sometimes ride in more comfort than the driver and fireman could provide. He was much loved by all the railway staff simply because he was so friendly. He would sit quietly by the driver and somehow never manage to impede his work or that of the numerous firemen who knew and loved him.

Jock regarded the Scottish Central Railway as his own particular railway, and Perth as his principal place of residence, but he made frequent trips to Aberdeen, Edinburgh, York and London. When he arrived at Perth station in the mornings – and he arrived ready to travel as often as three or four times per week – the staff simply patted him and let him through without a ticket. He would then simply choose whichever train took his fancy, climb aboard and wait for the off.

When he became really well known, drivers and firemen would be stricken at the sight of Jock climbing aboard someone else's train. On several occasions he got as far as Paris, where a Perth businessman recognised his familiar face. Three days later the businessman was in Lyon and there, resting on the main platform, was Jock.

Wherever he went, Jock always returned within a week or ten days to Perth but he was generally happy travelling each day with other commuters to Glasgow or Edinburgh. Once he travelled to London and vanished for nearly three weeks. Among the drivers and firemen there was talk of little else. Then a railway official spotted Jock in a rough-looking pet shop near King's Cross station in London. The official protested to the shop owner, who insisted he had come by Jock legitimately. There was nothing for it and the railway official bought Jock and only released him when they reached the station. As soon as he was let down on the platform Jock ran about in an ecstasy of tail-wagging and happy yelping. As soon as the Edinburgh express arrived he was greeted with cheers and pats by the crew before leaping aboard for the first part of his journey home.

When he died, the whole of the Scottish Central Railway went into mourning. It was estimated that his regular appearances around the station and his friendliness to everyone had actually made the Scottish Central Railway a more prosperous railway company than it would have been without Jock. It was even said that people booked their tickets partly to get where they wanted to go and partly to meet up with their old friend Jock once again. No one claimed the little body when it was found that he'd died quietly in his sleep and his passion for railways was never explained – all we know is that railways were the love of his life.

PRACTICAL JOKER

ENGLAND, 1890

The long-forgotten Victorian actor John Toole always travelled alone by train. This situation was forced on him because none of his friends and acquaintances would risk travelling with a man who was famous for his practical jokes. In his youth, these had been mild and reasonably funny but in later life his tricks had a crueller edge and were often hugely embarrassing or even painful for his victims.

Railway journeys more than cabs or coach journeys always brought out the worst in Toole: on one occasion he was travelling from London to Plymouth with a fellow actor called Southern. At some stage Toole managed to steal Southern's ticket while the poor man slept. Then, as they neared their station, Toole woke his companion and suggested they get their tickets, as the conductor was sure to demand them any minute.

Southern, of course, could not find his ticket and, as the poor man's panic increased, and his efforts to find the missing ticket became ever more frantic, Toole suggested that he hide under the seat. Now Southern was very particular about his dress, which was invariably immaculate, so he was not happy at the idea of lying on the dirty floor in a very tight space beneath his companion, but there seemed no other option, so he squeezed himself into the space and hoped for the best.

As soon as the conductor entered the carriage, Toole handed over his own ticket and then as the conductor was about to leave again, he said:

'Oh don't forget my friend.'

The conductor looking baffled replied: 'But where is he?'

'Oh, he's hiding under the seat,' came the reply.

Forced to travel on his own as a result of these and other escapades, Toole took to sleeping in the luggage racks or he would dress up as an African prince or a talkative old lady. But his most extraordinary exploit rebounded on him, to the eternal delight of his friends. He was travelling to Edinburgh, again with Southern – a very wary Southern, it must be added – and as the evening wore on he became rather bored. This was always a sign that some sort of a practical joke might be in the offing. Southern warned him not to try anything, but didn't try to intervene when Toole tried to remove the no smoking sign.

Toole couldn't do it, so he tried to dismantle the apparatus that held the oil lamp on the ceiling of the carriage. He managed to take it apart and then made the mistake of pushing his head up through the hole. He peered around in the gloom but, with the rush of the wind and the smoke and steam coming from the engine up ahead, found it rather uncomfortable. Clearly little sport was to be had with the oil lamps. So he tried to withdraw his head, but found he was stuck fast. Whether it was the shape of his head or the peculiar dimensions and construction of the hole no one knows, but having got his head in, he couldn't get it out again! He began to shout for help, but whether it was the noise of the train or the fact that Southern was rather tired and inattentive, Toole's cries were not heard and he had to travel for the next hour with his head sticking out of the top of the train. It was only the arrival of a ticket collector and a bar of slippery soap that eventually rescued the actor. His face was blackened and he was half-blinded by soot. Toole was furious that his cries had been ignored by Southern but Southern simply replied:

'I heard you but thought you were enjoying yourself – surely it was more fun than being in a luggage rack or perhaps under a seat?'

NOT MY STOP

ENGLAND, 1890

In Victorian times, and well into the twentieth century, there seems to have been an attitude of indifference to personal safety on the railway that today would seem astonishing. Partly this indifference had to do with the 'stiff upper lip' attitude that ran through all classes of society – there was a general horror at showing fear (and pretty much any other emotion) because such expressions were construed as weaknesses.

The attitude that was universally admired was that of cool, steely resilience – an attitude that led ultimately to the slaughter of so many young men in the trenches during the Great War. Railway accidents, which were frequent in the early days of train travel, produced numerous examples of the stiff upper lip attitude. One of the most extraordinary incidents occurred in the region covered by the Midland Railway company. In fact, Midland Railway staff dined out for years on the story. It concerned an old lady who was involved in a serious accident just outside Birmingham.

Two trains had collided at high speed. Their engines were smashed beyond repair and most of the carriages on both trains had come off the rails and toppled over. The carriage in which the old lady was travelling was one of the worst affected – it had rolled over several times as it fell to the bottom of a steep embankment.

As the dead and injured were released from the carriage, the old lady's voice was heard from somewhere deep within the tangled remains. The rescuers looked at each other and waited. Then, as they looked down, they saw the old lady crawl from beneath the wreckage.

211

'Is this Birmingham?' she asked.

'No, Ma'am, it's a catastrophe,' came the answer.

'Oh dear, dear,' said the old lady. 'Then I ought not to get off here.'

THE ITALIAN JOB

TURKEY, 1891

On 31 May 1891, the most famous train in the world – the *Orient Express* – was deliberately derailed. The gang who derailed the train then systematically robbed the passengers and took more than twenty hostages. The scene of the hold-up was near the Turkish village of Cherkeskui, and Greek bandits were immediately suspected as the culprits.

A rescue train was sent to the scene of the crime, but the Ottoman Empire was in its dying phase and so burdened with labyrinthine bureaucracy that it took twelve hours to agree to send the train and organise who would travel on it. Thus the train did not finally leave until many hours after the first reports of the outrage were received in Constantinople. When it did set off it went at a snail's pace, as the soldiers and officials on board were terrified that the track had been sabotaged and that in the dead of night they would not spot anything disastrous up ahead until it was too late and they had crashed into some deep ravine or swollen river.

At last the rescue train reached its destination and those passengers who had not been taken hostage were loaded aboard and taken to Constantinople. The train then turned round and went back again to the scene of the derailment, only this time carrying a team of railway engineers and lifting gear.

From interviews with the survivors, the authorities were able to build up a detailed picture of the incident. The driver had seen the torn track up ahead but had been unable to stop the train in time. He'd applied the brakes, however, which meant that the derailment was not nearly as serious as it might otherwise have been. The engine and the first few carriages had toppled down an embankment, and, as the dazed and bleeding passengers had climbed from the broken carriage windows, the remaining passengers (whose carriages had stayed on the tracks) spotted a gang of heavily armed men approaching rapidly on horseback. One said later that they had looked almost like comic book villains with large moustaches and dark capes, brandishing pistols and daggers.

When they dismounted, they began rounding up the men and women who had escaped from the derailed carriages. They tied up the driver and other railway company staff and left them lying face down at the side of the track.

The bandits ordered all the passengers out of the rest of the train (the part that had not been derailed) including those who had been asleep and were still undressed. The leader of the gang – all six-foot-four of him – had a huge black beard and demonic eyes. He told the terrified passengers that he would not kill anyone and that he was Anasthatos, leader of the Greek rebels.

He was festooned with daggers and guns but most of the passengers later insisted that he was enormously polite and charming. He ordered everyone to get back on to the carriages that had remained on the tracks and then ordered them to hand over all their valuables to his men. A passenger was shot in the arm by one bandit when he objected to handing over a personal item of jewellery. Immediately, Anasthatos ran along the corridor and knocked his fellow gang member to the ground before gently bandaging the injured man's arm. He then apologised for the incident and bowed to the injured man before returning to the other end of the train.

It was estimated that the gang got away with about $160,000 in money and jewels – several million in today's money. But the gang leader astonished everyone by handing back wedding rings and lockets to all the women!

Anasthatos then chose his hostages. He took the train driver, a British embassy official, several German businessmen and a number of the more obviously wealthy among the passengers.

After ordering the rest of the passengers to get back in the undamaged part of the train, he and his men disappeared into the dark night.

A day or so later one of the hostages arrived exhausted back at the scene of the derailment carrying a message from the kidnappers. He told officials that Anasthatos wanted £8,000 for the safe return of the passengers.

There was no point trying to find the gang as the countryside was wild and remote for hundreds of miles in every direction. The released hostages also made it clear that the gang would shoot their hostages if they were pursued.

Kaiser William II, outraged at the fact that German citizens were involved, threatened to invade with German troops. Terrified, the Turkish government came up with the £8,000 demanded by the gang.

Four men were sent by the gang leader to collect the money and they came with a letter explaining that if they were followed or impeded in any way when they set off on the return journey with the money then the hostages would be killed. Surrounded by soldiers and policemen, they took possession of the bags of gold and then set off for the gang's hideout. It took four days for the four men to reach the gang because the route they'd been given was deliberately circuitous, but they finally reached their destination and handed over the money. The hostages were immediately released unharmed. Anasthatos was never caught and got clean away with his loot.

RAILWAY HATERS

AMERICA, 1892

Many American train robbers were motivated as much by intense hatred of the railway as by the prospect of sudden riches. In fact, so widespread was the dislike of the iron road that the train robbers were often protected and cheered on by the ranchers. Of course, the vast distances across endless prairie also made catching the robbers far more difficult than it would have been in England or any other European country.

Among the most notorious of the early train-hating robbers were Chris Evans and John Sontag and the target of their attentions was the Southern Pacific Railway, which hauled vast sums of money through the gold-rush areas of the States.

The Southern Pacific was particularly reviled because many ranchers felt the company had taken their land – or crossed it – illegally, but, paradoxically, the railroad company was also accused of bypassing settlements that had argued about land prices.

Sontag and Evans were at heart disgruntled settlers out for money and revenge and, at the end of the nineteenth century, they set a new crime record for California. Using numerous, and sometimes hilarious disguises – huge red beards or Native American head-dress, for example – they would travel by train frequently in the run-up to a robbery. The disguises were adopted for the robberies themselves – the rest of the time the two men openly boasted about their life of crime and were regularly interviewed by the newspapers about it. In fact, such was their popularity and the unpopularity of the railway company that even the local sheriffs refused to arrest them! It was only when the government in Washington got wind of this outrageous lawlessness that something was finally done and the two flamboyant railway robbers were arrested, tried and sentenced to long prison terms.

ROYAL TRAIN

SCOTLAND, 1892

The Scots are famous for their spirit of independence from all things
English and they frequently take a delight in ignoring the sort of
spectacle that lesser mortals make a fuss about – particularly if it
has English connotations.

Which may explain why newspapers in Edinburgh took great
delight in publishing the comment of a young Scotsman who rushed
to Edinburgh Waverley station to see what all the fuss was about
when the Royal Train arrived one spring morning.

Crowds had gathered on the platform and back through the ticket
office out on to the street in the hope of getting a glimpse of Queen
Victoria. On the edge of the crowd and still on the street was a group
of newspapers reporters who'd been prevented from getting through
by the solid wall of people.

As they stood there a young man ran up and asked what all the
fuss was about. When he was told that the Queen was about to
arrive in the Royal Train he said: 'Is that all – I thought it was
something interesting, like a fight!'

TRIAL BY FIRE

AMERICA, 1892

The great difference between train journeys in the United States and train journeys in the UK can be summed up in one word: distance. And of course, when the Wild West was first opened up at the end of the nineteenth century the railway engineers had to cope with difficult terrain, angry Native Americans, outlaws, and a huge territory that had only minimal policing and infrastructure.

This led to a situation in which, at times, and on certain journeys, there was only a fifty-fifty chance that you would reach your destination unscathed. If the train wasn't attacked by native tribes the tracks might have been ripped up by angry settlers or washed away by flood and tempest.

Among the more unusual hazards to which rail travellers were once subjected was fire. On one journey through the mid-West in the 1890s for more than a hundred miles the train had to run through a prairie that was on fire from horizon to horizon. For the nearly three hours it took to pass through the flames the passengers were asked to wear blankets previously soaked in water. They were also asked to keep looking out the windows in case the paint began to blister on the sides of the carriages or even burst into flame. When this happened buckets of water were passed down the corridors and tipped out the window over the fire, wherever it happened to be. In this way, the train managed to get through the burning prairie without mishap. The only difficulty was that the passengers were exhausted and covered in

219

wet soot by the time they arrived at their destination. But then, as one man was heard to comment: 'It wasn't near damn as dangerous as travelling out west in the old stage coach days!'

BLOOD ON THE TRACKS

PALESTINE, 1892

The opening of a new railway was always a time for rejoicing wherever and whenever it occurred. But of course, the exact nature of the celebrations surrounding an opening ceremony would vary greatly from country to country and from culture to culture. Appeasing the local gods was important, as the opening of the Jaffa to Jerusalem Railway reveals.

Jerusalem station was completely covered with palm branches on the great day and the Turkish cavalry – with drawn swords – kept a way open through the surging crowds for the officials and their guests. The railway was opened according to strict Muslim rites. Three unfortunate white sheep with gilded horns were dragged on to the rails and then slaughtered, prior to which an Imam, dressed in green robes and a green turban, offered up a prayer.

When the sheeps' veins had been emptied the carcasses were taken away by a group of soldiers and the train advanced slowly over the blood-drenched rails, after which, the line now being considered free of the influence of evil genii, the officials got into the compartments reserved for them. Here they sat on large cushions on the floor with the ceiling of the carriage above their heads draped in silks and carpets and numerous other rich and gaudy hangings.

Three guns were fired and the train at last set off into the fierce desert heat.

CLAIMS FOR DAMAGES

ENGLAND, 1892

It wasn't long after railway travel became widely available that the railway companies realised that they would need to be insured if they were to survive claims for damages following accidents. With the best will in the world, they knew that however many safety precautions were put in place accidents were bound still to happen now and then and, without insurance, the claims of injured passengers could easily put a company out of business. But word quickly spread that injured passengers were receiving substantial sums of money and numerous fraudulent claims were uncovered over the years. On at least one occasion, a man sitting on a railway embankment spotted a derailment half a mile away and immediately ran to the scene of the accident. He rolled around in the spilled oil and dirt, tore his clothes and knocked his head against a few twisted pieces of metal. He later made a claim against the railway company and received more than £100 in compensation – a considerable sum in the 1870s. He was only found out when a policeman overheard him boasting about his new-found wealth in a local pub.

The most extraordinary example of a false claim for an accident concerned a woman who travelled regularly in the 1890s on the Southern Region. She sued the railway company for injuries sustained when she slipped on the platform while running for a train.

When the case came to court, a railway official thought the woman looked rather familiar and, through the railway's lawyers, he managed to get the judge to give him more time to conduct investigations. After some skilful detective work he established that this was the fourth accident for which the company had been asked to pay this particular woman and on the last occasion she had been awarded a very large sum of money as a result of total and permanent paralysis!

When the judge heard the new evidence he dismissed the case and warned the woman never again to waste the court's time or she might well end up behind bars.

PIN AND LINK MEN

AMERICA, 1893

In the USA, before auto couplers (a device that locked the two carriages together automatically) were invented, a group of brave souls known as the pin and link men put the carriages together to make a train. It was a very dangerous job and almost every pin and link man had at some stage – if his career lasted long enough – lost a finger or two. Men who stuck the job for a decade or more might end up with hands mangled beyond all recognition.

The difficulty was that the links – one on the end of each carriage – had to be aligned by the pin and link man even as the two carriages moved together. Once the couplings or links were correctly positioned, the pin and link man pushed his pin home, but a sudden movement by the engine just at the critical moment could easily trap a finger or thumb. Towards the end of 1893 one old pin and link man went to see the train master after losing his last finger. The loss of that digit meant he could no longer do the job; he hoped to be taken on in some other capacity but the train master simply dismissed him – nineteenth-century America was clearly a tough, not to say brutal, place. But if conditions were tough the men themselves were tougher. Despite his mangled hands and the loss of his livelihood the pin and link man still managed a joke. The train master asked him if he could recommend a replacement – someone who could carry on making up the trains.

'You probably want someone who'd last longer than me. I've got just the man. You need old Johnny Rogan who works in the yards downtown.'

224

'What's so good about him?' said the train master.

'Oh he's got six fingers on each hand anyways – he'll last plenty longer than me!'

JUST A QUICK ONE

ENGLAND, 1894

It took nearly three years before regular commuters on all the main lines out of London – to the north-east, north-west, south, south-east and south-west – became aware of something slightly odd. When the rumours spread and an investigation had been set up by the railway companies, the pieces quickly came together and it was established that the bizarre confidence trick had begun two and a half years earlier on commuter trains leaving Euston in the evenings.

Just as the train was about to leave, a well-spoken young man was seen running along the platform shouting up at passengers through the open windows.

'A woman has fainted – does anyone have any brandy or whisky?'

Invariably – this being the 1890s – someone would have a hip flask and it would be handed down.

'That's terribly kind. I'll just go and administer a dose and be right back.'

The young man dashed back along the platform like some latter-day Sir Galahad. But the elderly gentleman who'd handed over his hip flask waited in vain for it to be returned. He spoke to the guard and the ticket collector. Neither knew a thing about a woman fainting.

It was assumed that this, the first victim of the hip-flask trickster as he became known, was not a victim at all. The ticket collector reassured the elderly passenger that in the rush to bring help to a woman in distress his hip flask had probably not been returned simply because the woman had to be taken off the train and the young man had accompanied her.

Over the coming months the same or a similar trick was carried out on trains about to leave King's Cross, Liverpool Street, Victoria and Waterloo. The young man escaped detection because he carried out his little deception only once every two weeks and each time at a different station. But then he became overconfident and his hit rate increased to once, sometimes twice a week.

He was finally arrested when a passenger remembered a similar earlier incident. The passenger reported his suspicions to the guard, who collared the young man as he headed towards the station entrance. The police later found thirty silver flasks at the young man's home, but it was suspected that he'd already sold on many more.

HINTS TO RAILWAY TRAVELLERS

IRELAND, 1896

A Dublin man whom the newspapers of the time recorded only by his initials, G F G, had clearly grown weary of his fellow railway travellers because he began a campaign of bill sticking on train and station walls that was both bizarre and amusing. Having made numerous complaints about the loud, boisterous and completely inconsiderate behaviour typical of the passengers on a particular line – and one used regularly by G F G – he drew up and had published in poster form a number of hints and suggestions for, as he put it, 'the august consideration of those travellers not yet well versed in the correct mode of behaviour to be adopted during a railway journey'.

The posters were for many months displayed throughout the Irish railway system, though no one ever saw them being put up. They read as follows:

In the event of the carriage being crowded, always insist on keeping as much of your luggage as possible inside. Don't whatever happens offer to put a scrap of it in the luggage van. There is a special place for trunks, etc., but don't let this disturb your equanimity – put your trunk on any available seat and that way you will keep your luggage close at hand and also enjoy the privacy of your own company. Should you be gifted with a voice suggestive of the melody of a consumptive foghorn, or a falsetto articulation, always give your vocal organs full scope, and relieve the ample reservoir of your loquacity by retailing all the inane gossip and petty scandals at your command.

In regard to the topics most calculated to delight your fellow travellers, that, of course, entirely rests with yourself – the platform is yours. That you are acquainted with certain members of the Royal Family goes without saying; at the same time you should not be oblivious of the fact that other people will enjoy hearing you cough and splutter, you should also expectorate as often as possible and blow smoke into the four corners of your compartment. If your fellow travellers are particularly sensitive or elderly, try to use as much abusive language as you can muster; eat noisily, throw your rubbish on the compartment floor. In this way you will be following in the great traditions of railway travel in this beautiful island of ours.

THE FLAGGING MAN

AMERICA, 1897

A railroad in South Carolina was being sued after one of its trains struck a carriage on a highway crossing and killed four people. The case went to trial and the lawyers for the prosecution called many witnesses, among whom was the flagman at the railway crossing where the accident occurred. He was cross-examined as follows:

Q: What is your name?

A: Henry Johnson Rufus Lee.

Q: Mr Lee, I want you to tell me just what you were doing on the night of August 3rd, the date of the accident.

A: I was flagging on the crossing.

Q: You were flagging on the crossing?

A: Yes, sir.

Q: Well, now, what happened?

A: Well, the number ten come down an' struck the carriage and killed four people.

Q: What were you doing at the time?

A: I was flagging.

Q: What were you flagging with?

A: I was flagging with a lantern.

Q: What kind of a lantern did you have? Was it a white lantern or a red lantern?

A: I had a red lantern.

Q: Now, Mr Lee, tell me what kind of a night it was – was it a dark night or a bright moonlight night?

A: It was a very dark night, sir.

Q: Now are you sure it was not a bright moonlit night?

A: No, sir, very dark.

Q: Now, you say you were flagging with a red lantern?

A: Yes, sir.

Q: Are you sure you were not flagging with a white lantern?

A: Yes, sir.

Q: Now, I want you to be very positive; you say it was a very dark night, and that you were flagging with a red lantern?

A: Yes, sir, I was flagging with a red lantern.

The following day the president of the railway sent for the flagman and said, 'Mr Lee, I want to present you with this cheque to show our appreciation of the evidence that you gave at the trial yesterday. It was clear and conclusive.'

Rufus Lee took the cheque and said, 'My, my, Mr President, I never had so much money in my life, but I was very nervous yesterday. That lawyer man kept asking me, was it a bright moonlight night, or was it a dark night? And did I have a white lantern, or did I have a red lantern? I thought for sure he was a-going to ask me if that lantern was lit!'

JUSTICE BY RAIL

WALES, 1898

Today, businessmen and others regularly work on the train as they travel to and from work or on longer journeys around the country or even around the world. The fact that work is possible while travelling has always made the train an attractive option compared with, say, the car. But work of a far wider variety once took place on many railway journeys. One of the strangest examples occurred in South Wales, where a carriage was turned into an official law court.

It all began when Judge Williams, who had been trying a case in Bridgend County Court, found that he could not finish it on the same day. One important witness had still to be examined when the court rose. The judge knew he could not continue in the morning because he was due at another court first thing next day and the other court was many miles away.

Determined not to put the parties to the case to the expense of what would have proved a lengthy adjournment, the judge suggested a plan to the barristers involved and then rushed off to the station, where he was joined in the carriage by the lawyers, the defendant (suitably accompanied) and the important witness.

As the train pursued its journey the witness gave his evidence and was cross-examined at some length by both barristers. Instead of adjourning for lunch, the 'court' simply waited until the train reached a station with a decent café and then dashed in for a sandwich and tea. The barrister sat between the judge and the defendant over lunch, but later remarked that he found the whole proceeding far more enjoyable and conducive to justice than the stuffy confines of the traditional courtroom restaurant.

When the train reached its destination, the whole party alighted and set off for the stationmaster's office, where the judge delivered his verdict.

BIG WOMAN

CANADA, 1898

Certain railway jobs have always attracted men of a thoughtful cast of mind. The signalman's trade is a good example. Many signal boxes were in extremely remote places where there might only be a few trains each day. In between trains, as it were, the signalman had time to think. Many were great readers; others kept detailed accounts of all they saw around them, at least one mended clocks and another built a canoe.

Porters, drivers and firemen inevitably had less time to record what was going on but at least one booking office clerk – a Canadian – wrote a regular column for his local newspaper about the odd characters he and his fellow booking office clerks came across now and then in the line of duty.

His favourite tale, which was recorded by him in 1898, concerned what he rather unkindly referred to as 'a vigorous lady of the elephantine type'.

She appeared at the ticket gate of a Canadian Pacific Railway station and asked for a ticket to Vankleek Hill.

The booking office clerk on duty that day – not the recorder of the tale – was a thin, pallid-faced man. When the rather large woman asked for her ticket the clerk enquired laconically: 'Single?'

With a look of withering scorn and resentment the woman replied:

'It ain't none of your business whether I'm single, married or a widder. I might have been married a dozen times or more if I had felt like providing for a lazy, shiftless, good fer nothin' shrivelled-up bit of a man like you!'

He sold her a single.

GHOULISH PASSENGER

ENGLAND, 1898

One of the greatest difficulties with railway travel is that one cannot easily choose one's companions. Most travellers, of course, fit well within the broad range of what might be described as fairly ordinary and we therefore barely notice them when we share a carriage; those few who seem a little more eccentric or outlandish or even threatening than the norm represent a far smaller group but these are the people we remember.

Today, when most trains have open plan carriages with perhaps fifty or more people seated in them, the influence of eccentric characters is somewhat diluted but, in the days when carriages were made up of small compartments got up pretty much like the old stage coaches, things were very different.

A Sussex newspaper reported in the 1890s the experience of a young but rather timid mother who entered a compartment on the early morning train from Brighton to London. She had made herself and her child comfortable by the window and, hearing the whistle that indicated the train's imminent departure, was looking forward to having the carriage to herself, when a tall and very gloomy individual entered her compartment and shut the door. He sat down and stared fixedly ahead. She later described his complexion as white to the point of death and explained how her discomfort increased dramatically when, to her cheerful 'Good morning,' he returned only a mournful stare.

She decided that a journey to London with such a man almost opposite her was more than she could endure, but she was reluctant to move to another compartment after feeling so pleased with herself at having discovered this one empty. But how could she get rid of him? Then, just as she was about to give up and move, she had an idea: she decided to be courageous and tell a white lie.

She leaned across to her fellow traveller and said in a loud and determined voice:

'I just thought I ought to tell you that my little girl here has only just recovered from a dreadful attack of scarlet fever and I fear she is still highly infectious.'

'Oh don't worry about me, mum,' interrupted the man, 'I'm committing suicide when we get to the first tunnel.'

The horrified woman packed her things, clutched her child to her bosom and changed compartments. The next passenger who joined the gloomy man might have noticed that he had cheered up no end. Needless to say, he did not commit suicide when the train reached the first tunnel.

BLACKWALL DRAG

ENGLAND, 1899

When the very first passengers boarded the London and Blackwall Railway they were about to travel on what even today must count as one of the most bizarre railways ever built.

The railway was worked not by steam engines that moved along the track pulling the carriages, but by stationary engines fixed at either end of the route. A rope was attached to the fixed engines and this was used to drag the carriages along the rail. There was rope for the up and another for the down traffic, each rope having a total length of about eight miles and a weight of 40 tons. And on this line one of the earliest electric telegraph systems was used to tell the engineer at Blackwall or Fenchurch Street when to begin to wind up or let go his rope.

On that first journey the down train, as it left Fenchurch Street, consisted of seven carriages. The two carriages at the front went through to Blackwall; the next carriage only as far as Poplar, the next to the next station and so to the seventh carriage, which was left behind at Shadwell, the first station after leaving Fenchurch Street. As the train approached Shadwell, the guard, who had to stand on a rickety platform in front of the carriage, pulled out a pin from the coupling just in time to allow the momentum of the carriage to allow it to carry on sufficiently far to ensure that it stopped in the right place.

The same process was repeated at each subsequent station, till finally the two remaining carriages ran up the terminal incline, and were brought to a stand at the Blackwall station. On the return

238

journey the carriage at each station was attached to the rope at a fixed hour, and then the whole series were set in motion simultaneously, so that they arrived at Fenchurch Street at intervals proportional to the distance between the stations.

There were perpetual delays, owing to the rope breaking, and the cost of repairs and renewals was huge – so much so that within a few years of its inauguration the system was abandoned.

LANGUAGE DIFFICULTIES

INDIA, 1899

A tea planter and his family were late arriving at the station for the train that was to take them away from the stifling heat of summer in Bombay to the cool of the north and the slopes of the Himalayas. The Raj was still unquestioned at this time and of course Europeans were always treated as a cut above the rest, so the family – a father and his two daughters – was allowed to board the train without buying their tickets.

However, the tea planter's confident assertion that the family would pay at the other end of their journey was taken with a pinch of salt by the booking office clerk. Like all good Indian bureaucrats he did things by the book and as soon as the train carrying the family north had steamed out of the station he wired ahead to the booking office at the other end of the line.

His telegraph message, which became famous throughout the Indian Railway Service, ran as follows: 'Obtain fares. Three Europeans travelling first class sleeping compartment in night attire. One adult and two adultresses.'

FAITHFUL SERVANT

ENGLAND, 1930

In June 1930, Tom Holton's father was stationmaster at Towcester and the family lived in the station house. When Tom's sister died in an epidemic, the railway company put on a special train to carry the coffin and mourners to their ancestral home at the village of Slapton, five miles away.

The train waited at the nearest point to the church while bearers carried the coffin half a mile along a field path to the churchyard where the burial took place. The track was a single line so no other train could pass. The family were then conveyed back to Towcester.

The train company, the Stratford-upon-Avon and Midland Junction Railway, was more than once in the receiver's hands, but it was not too poor to pay this compliment to a faithful servant.

SPIKED

CANADA, 1900

The General Superintendent of the Canadian Pacific Railway dismounted from his private carriage and walked down the track to where the gang were renewing the sleepers. They had finished their work on the piece of track over which he had to travel in order to reach the foreman. As luck would have it, on his way he found a track spike that appeared to have been abandoned. He was a stickler for order and tidiness and seeing the abandoned spike roused him to a fury. When he got within hailing distance of the foreman he shouted: 'How often must you be told not to leave any scrap material scattered over the right-of-way? Look at this spike I have just picked up.'

Now the foreman, an Irishman, was reputed to be the wittiest man on the railway. In a battle of words he was never beaten and where wit failed he could normally charm his way out of any awkward situation. He looked calmly at the General Superintendent and said: 'Well, if that don't beat all!' Then, waving vigorously to the gang of ten men, he shouted, 'Come here, the lot of ye; here's this damned spike we hunted fer all yesterday afternoon and couldn't find at all, but the General Sooprintindint has jist found it! Isn't it yourself sir, that has the eagle eye.'

The General Superintendent knew when he was beaten. He smiled, turned on his heel and set off back the way he'd come without another word.

On another occasion a Mr Fraser, the owner of most of the railway company, found himself in his private carriage but stuck out on a siding. He was bored so he got out to stretch his legs. The famously witty old Irishman was tapping the wheels. The official went up to him and said: 'Morning. How do you like the wheels?'

'Not worth a damn,' was the reply.

'Well, how do you like the carriage?'

'It's good enough for the wheels,' came the reply.

'What do you think of the railroad?'

'It matches the carriage.'

Fraser looked at the old chap for a minute and said:

'Do you know who I am?'

'Shure I do,' retorted the old man. 'You're young Fraser, and I knew your father when he was president of the road, and by God, he's going to be president of it again.'

'Why, my father is dead,' said Fraser.

'I know that, and the road is going to hell,' was the reply.

BLOCKING THE TRACKS

AMERICA, 1900

At one stage in the nineteenth century, American railroad companies employed so many conductors that passengers' tickets were clipped, stamped and punched, it seemed, every few miles. This over-manning developed gradually in response to the railroad owners' almost obsessive desire to catch all those who travelled without buying a ticket. Soon the costs of preventing fraud, largely the costs of extra ticket inspectors, hugely outweighed the benefits – it just wasn't worth it and by the time the railroad company realised their mistake there were an awful lot of people to be got rid of. No one likes to lose their job, but railroad staff who'd expected a job for life were in some cases very angry indeed when they discovered they were to be laid off.

One conductor was so furious that he paid a group of his friends to block the track with a pile of old sleepers. It was on a section where the train didn't travel so fast that there were likely to be many fatalities, but when the engine and three carriages came off the track, the conductor – who was on the very train he'd deliberately sabotaged – refused to help in any way. He sat on a rock nearby and when asked why he didn't do his duty and try to restore some order to the chaos he merely replied: 'They damn well laid me off I want to see how they like it now! They want to do without me? *Now* they can damn well do without me!'

244

WICKED TONGUE

ENGLAND, 1900

The guard on a train was once vitally important. He literally guarded the train and its passengers while the driver got on with the more straightforward business of keeping the thing moving. Until relatively recently, guards used a hand brake to assist the vacuum brakes applied by the driver and they kept an eye on the passengers and carriages to see that there were no problems.

Guards tended to be a law unto themselves and they would take no nonsense from other railway employees, whether they be drivers, managers or even at times directors.

A famously bad-tempered guard on the Great Northern Railway became something of a legend: he'd been known to box the ears of cheeky boys; he would intervene if he felt young ladies were reading unsuitable magazines or novels and on several occasions he found someone smoking in a non-smoking compartment and put them off the train at the next station. He once ejected a foreign diplomat for this offence and, when the spluttering and indignant smoker threatened to contact the guard's superiors, the guard shouted back 'I ain't got any superiors!'

But this guard of the old school could also be charming and amusing. He was much loved by regular passengers, who enjoyed listening to him sing famous operatic arias, and he was a famous wit. Perhaps his greatest sally came when he found a passenger leaning out of the window.

'Put your head inside, sir,' he shouted to the passenger as the train steamed out of the station.

'I shall do as I like,' retorted the passenger.

'All right,' came the reply. 'Do as you please, but you must understand that you'll be held liable for all damage done to the stonework of the company's bridges.'

AN EXTRAORDINARY ESCAPE

ENGLAND, 1903

Many hair's-breadth escapes from almost certain death have been recorded in the annals of railway history, one of the most wonderful being that of the man who, in the early days of corridor trains, stepped out on the wrong side of a Great Western express running at 60 miles per hour, and alighted on the tracks without receiving a scratch.

Passengers unused to the idea of corridors often made the mistake of choosing the wrong side of a compartment, particularly if it was late at night or they'd had a few drinks – in fact, the railway companies became so worried about the problem that for a while, on some trains they put up signs saying 'Corridor this way!'

Almost more marvellous than the man who hit the tracks at 60 miles per hour and lived to tell the tale was the case of Messrs Hussey (father and son) who, while crossing the line at Round Oak Station, on 14 March 1903, were run over by an engine and van. Witnesses said later that the two men were right in the path of the engine when they were hit and could not – should not – have survived, since even a glancing blow from an engine would be enough in most cases to cause instant death.

In the case of the father and son, the engine was fitted with a water scoop, which left less than a foot of space between it and the ground, and yet the two men were practically unhurt, and travelled by the train for which they had booked. The incidents of their arrival at the station, hair's-breadth escape, and departure by train were crowded into the space of a few minutes.

PHILANTHROPIST ON THE TRAIN

ENGLAND, 1903

From the very beginning, trains have exerted a strange pull on a certain percentage of the population. This percentage is almost exclusively male and highly prone to making lists. We don't know when the earliest train spotters appeared on the scene but it's certain that within a few years of railway services being established young men and old became fascinated by them. For most, this fascination took the form of recording sightings of particular trains or learning everything there was to know about how engines were made and routes established. But one remarkable man found trains so compelling that they made him give a great deal of his money away.

It all began innocently enough. An elderly woman travelling on the Great Western Region for her annual holiday in Cornwall was approached by the ticket collector and told that she'd been invited to dine in the first-class dining carriage. When she protested that she was quite happy to eat her sandwiches, the guard explained that an elderly gentleman would be enormously grateful if she would have lunch at his expense. Unable to resist the temptation, she enjoyed what she later described as the best meal of her life. But, when she approached the ticket collector and asked if she might meet and thank her benefactor, he explained that the elderly gentleman was virtually a recluse and found meeting new people extremely difficult.

Similar incidents occurred pretty frequently over the coming months and the story reached the local newspapers. Who on earth was this elderly eccentric who kept buying other elderly people expensive lunches? No one knew. Then there was a further development. Ticket collectors reported being asked to offer passengers cash and cheques – not for huge sums but enough to make a real difference. In each case the recipient appeared down on his or her luck and in each case the intermediary was a ticket collector. The wealthy reclusive train traveller would never meet those to whom he gave but he did pass on the same message each time he made a donation. He would always say – and each time through the ticket collector – 'I hope you have enjoyed your journey and that this money will persuade you again in the future to travel on the greatest transport invention ever made.'

It was only when a startled beneficiary was asked to describe which ticket collector had passed on the message and the cheque that railway officials realised what had been happening. The ticket collector was described as stout and red-faced with a thick head of white hair. It just happened that the ticket collector on this particular train was one of the best known on the GWR and he bore absolutely no relation to the description. The eccentric philanthropist had been impersonating a ticket collector, but after the story appeared in the local newspapers the eccentric ticket collector was never seen or heard of again. His identity was never discovered.

DREAMING DRIVER

AMERICA, 1903

A well-known American engine driver, with 25 years' experience, had been involved in a dozen or more accidents in which his locomotive was overturned or derailed. Each time he had dreamed beforehand of the accident, seeing in the dream the exact place, the direction in which the train was going, and the side on which the engine was overturned. At various times his dreams came early enough and with sufficient detail to prevent collisions; over a number of years local newspapers credited him with saving many lives and much property in this way.

He recorded one of his extraordinary experiences in a specially written feature for a long-forgotten newspaper.

At one time I was in charge of a construction train, being driver, conductor and gang-boss combined. One night I saw in a dream the collision of an express with a through freight train at the station where I stopped. The engines and coaches were badly smashed up and many killed and wounded. The dream was very vivid and distressed me all the next day. The second morning my train was ready to start, but the through freight, which was late, came along, passing the station within seven minutes of the express train, a very reckless thing, as it was in a cutting which had a sharp curve, through which the express always came at full speed. At that very moment, to my horror I heard the whistle of the express. It recalled my dream at once.

Seizing the red flag, I signalled the freight train, and ran down the curve to flag the express, whose driver reversed at once, and the engines came to a halt within ten feet of each other.

As it was not my duty to flag other trains, or to pay any attention to them, had it not been for the dream and its effects on my mind, causing me to be doubly on the alert at that time, there would have been a serious collision, as the express had nine very full coaches. Some considered it a lucky coincidence, but these, in my experience, have been too frequent, and the dreams too real for me to consider them as such.

MOBBED BY MAGPIES

RUSSIA, 1903

Oliver Ready travelled through Siberia and Manchuria (now in China) by rail in 1903. His account of the journey is filled with fascinating details. When the train, leaving Germany and entering Russia, stopped at the border town of Alexandrowo, for example, the Russian officials stood at one end of the platform staring malevolently at the German officials at the other. Neither side would speak to the other. The Russians wore white smocks down to the ground, the Germans stiff, uncomfortable uniforms of the Kaiser's army. At the railway hotel in Warsaw, Ready could hardly eat his dinner because the dining room was so bright. An official later told him it was lit by more than a thousand gaslights.

The trans-Siberian railway was hugely overcrowded throughout its long journey and passports were demanded all hours of the day and night – sometimes as often as a dozen times in one night. Despite having a first-class ticket, Ready had to sleep on top of the huge piles of luggage that littered every surface area – carriage floors, seats, and beds. In a compartment designed for two he found nine people sleeping.

During the 5,000-mile journey Ready met a most remarkable man. He had never left his small Siberian village, yet his English was perfect and he was a huge fan of Jane Austen and of Hampshire's chalkstream trout fishing! For two days Ready listened to an extraordinary stream of anecdotes, first about *Emma* or *Pride and Prejudice*, then about the best dry fly for the Itchen or Test at certain times of year.

The rather one-sided conversation only came to an end when they reached a station at which a vast volley of gunfire was heard. Ready stuck his head out of a window and discovered several hundred soldiers lined up along the platform firing continually into the air. No one seemed to know why. And at the next station, where the train waited for several hours, a group of bedraggled men, women and children were marched behind a wall at gunpoint by a group of soldiers. This was followed by the sound of shooting and then the soldiers reappeared but without the group of civilians. Ready was terribly shocked but the other passengers merely shrugged.

As Ready's extraordinary journey reached its end the train was mobbed by thousands of magpies and, for the last 100 miles, there was an armed Chinese guard stationed every 100 yards by the side of the tracks.

MAKE ME RICH

AMERICA, 1904

John Stevens was the porter on local passenger trains between Los Angeles and San Francisco. While travelling on the train one day, his best friend – also a railway worker – asked for a loan of $200, which Stevens let him have, taking as security a silver watch and a mortgage on a 40-acre tract of land.

Railwaymen stick together and Stevens felt he had to help a fellow porter, despite his misgivings. They travelled together by train to discuss the details of the loan and, when Stevens finally decided to hand over the money, he could not have imagined that the decision would at first cause him untold grief and then bring him untold riches. 'It was the train journey of a lifetime,' he later said. 'A journey that nearly broke me and then made me for life!'

But at the time, that was all in the future. In the meantime, when the loan repayment was due, Stevens' friend was unable to pay, the mortgage was foreclosed, and Stevens had no choice but to buy an apparently worthless piece of land. He tried to auction off the land, but without success. Then one day, while waiting for the 12.10, a little man whom he had noticed watching him for some time tapped him on the shoulder as he stood on the platform and asked, 'Is your name Stevens?'

'Yes, sir,' came the reply.

'You own 40 acres of land in Texas?'

'Yes, sir, I do indeed.'

'I will give you $5,000 for it.'

The amount was so large it staggered Stevens, but he was a cool,

254

shrewd fellow and told the man he would think about it. He believed so strongly in the benign influence of the railway that in order to think about this apparently amazing offer he decided to take a long railway journey.

When he arrived back at his home station, the same man was waiting for him. He said. 'See here, I'll tell you what I'll do: if you will give me a bill of sale now I will pay you $10,000.'

That settled it. Stevens knew that the decision he'd made on his journey was the right one – he was not going to sell. He made up his mind that the 40 acres must contain something of extraordinary value.

He told the stranger that under no consideration would he sell then, but would decide in a few days. On arriving at the end of his run he got two days' leave of absence and went to his farm, where he found that a big oil gusher had broken loose. The result was, he left the railroad, organised a company, retaining a controlling interest, and within a few months he was a multimillionaire.

He never lost his love of railways and later built the most luxurious Pullman carriage ever seen. He travelled in it regularly for the rest of his life just to feel again the rattle of the wheels beneath him.

CHANCE MEETING

IRELAND, 1905

For many years, Sir Arthur Chance was acting medical adviser to the Irish Railway company. He was continually astonished at the tricks passengers would get up to in order to squeeze compensation money out of the railway authorities. Among the more bizarre claims was one from a farmer who insisted his prize cattle failed to produce enough calves each year as a result of stress caused by the passage of trains across his land; an elderly woman put in a huge claim for compensation after explaining in a long but rather mysterious letter that her daughter's marriage prospects had been ruined after an encounter with what she described as 'a non-European' on one of the company's trains.

But the incident on which Sir Arthur dined out most concerned a cattle dealer. The man had been travelling on the midnight train from Dublin to Belfast. The train was derailed and several coaches over-turned. Many of the passengers were injured but luckily not fatally.

The cattle dealer's writ for damages against the railway company was received a few days later and Sir Arthur was called in to advise. He decided to visit the cattle dealer. He found that he was indeed badly injured and so he advised the railway company to make an immediate settlement. The railway made an offer and to their great surprise it was immediately accepted.

Some time later Sir Arthur happened to be once more in the cattle dealer's neighbourhood. He thought he would call on the man, see how he was progressing and ask, in passing, why the cattle dealer had accepted the first offer made by the railway company.

He was astonished to discover that the cattle dealer was fully recovered. In the course of their conversation and, anxious to clear up the point that had long puzzled him, Sir Arthur asked why the injured dealer had accepted the first offer made.

'Well, between you me and the gatepost,' said the man, 'I was travelling without a ticket!'

A MAN IN A DRESS

FRANCE, 1905

Before the Great War, passports were hardly necessary, at least in Europe. Those few wealthy individuals who could afford to travel simply got on a boat and got off on the other side of the Channel or the North Sea. Customs officials might harass them over wine or tobacco duties but that was about it. The fact that the vast majority of Europeans never travelled anywhere can be attributed to the fact that the travel industry and the low cost travel it made possible did not yet exist.

This lack of interchange between countries also meant, of course, that we knew less about each other's cultures than we do now. Most villagers had never left the place where they were born and grew up, which meant, for example, that in remote rural parts of Greece the national costume was at least in part still worn and men looked pretty much like Elizabethan courtiers in their doublet and hose. Television and the ubiquitous use of English had yet to make them realise that the rest of the world was not as they were.

The lack of awareness of other people's cultures led occasionally to embarrassment, hilarity or both, as a gentleman from Scotland discovered while travelling through rural France by train. He had travelled down from his native Edinburgh with no problems, for Queen Victoria had made all things Scottish highly fashionable, and our traveller believed that the habits and dress of Scotland should be better known right across Europe. He had therefore donned kilt, sporran and dirk before setting out on his long train journey to the South of France.

Having crossed the Channel all went well. He slept till he reached Paris, changed trains and continued on his way. He did arouse astonishment in Paris but it was kept within bounds and amounted to little more than a bit of pointing and a few open mouths. But, as the train for the south travelled through the more rustic regions of rural France, this situation changed. At last the train stopped at a remote station and two elderly, respectable and highly religious ladies entered the Scotsman's carriage. At first all went well, for the Scotsman was asleep under a blanket. But at last he woke and stood up to leave the carriage in order to stretch his legs in the corridor. At once the two elderly Frenchwomen began to scream and shout. The Scotsman stood dumbfounded until the guard, breathless in his haste, entered the compartment. The two women, still in an almost hysterical rage, demanded the removal of the pervert in petticoats. The guard, who knew a great deal about the world and had travelled widely for his job, pointed out that the Scotsman was simply dressed in the costume of his country.

The Frenchwomen were unmoved. 'To ride with a man in a dress!' They almost spat the words. 'It is impossible, *incroyable,* it is not proper, not even decent.' They told the guard that unless something was done they would pull the communication cord the instant the train left the station. There was nothing for it. The guard helped the two women carry their luggage to a first-class compartment and the look of satisfaction on their faces when they arrived at their new seats seemed somehow not entirely attributable to their escape from the man in petticoats.

RAILWAY WIT

ENGLAND, 1906

Railway staff were famous at one time for their sardonic wit. This probably had to do with the fact that they were constantly dealing with a largely indifferent or ungrateful public. But the public ultimately paid their wages and senior staff would not tolerate sharp words to the travelling public even where the travelling public probably deserved it.

The only way round the problem was to learn to respond in ways that enabled the staff to let off steam while leaving the public unsure whether they had been ticked off or not.

Wit was also a vital tool for relationships between staff and, as in many jobs and professions, railway people had countless 'in jokes' and sayings that outsiders would have found baffling. Among the legendary conversations re-told endlessly was the one between a stationmaster, a customer – in this case the customer had sent a parcel by rail – a porter and a booking clerk.

The stationmaster was famous for tolerating no other opinion than his own and was therefore always right. Early one morning he found himself in the thick of a dispute about why and how exactly a parcel sent by train had been damaged. The sender declared that the breakages were due to the carelessness of the porter handling them, while the porter was highly indignant at the suggestion and called attention to the fact that the box was badly packed.

'I expect, if the truth's known,' said the booking clerk, putting in his oar, 'it was six of one and half a dozen of the other.'

'You weren't asked for your opinion, Mr Jenkins,' snapped the stationmaster, irritably. 'And as it happens, you're quite wrong – it was just the opposite.'

But real wit among railway men could come from the youngest members of staff as a little snippet from an East London local paper of the Edwardian era reveals.

The railway company had been taking on new van boys at the goods depot, and among the applicants was a smart little Cockney lad. The little lad reached the front of the queue and was interviewed by the gaffer.

'What's your name?' asked the gaffer.

' 'Arry Coggins, sir.'

'Where do you live?' came the next query.

'Lambeth, sir.'

'Lambeth, eh? Have you lived there all your life?'

'No, not yet, sir,' came the prompt retort.

WHISKY BARREL

SCOTLAND, 1906

Life is always difficult for the churchman who likes to drink. In the Anglican and Catholic churches drinking in moderation is just about tolerated, but among the stricter protestant sects, particularly the Presbyterians, the very idea of drink is anathema. Which creates the curious paradox that the country that produces some of the most delicious alcoholic drink in the world – namely Scotland – also produces some of the strictest Presbyterians.

Occasionally drink and Presbyterianism do battle and drink is invariably the winner. A classic case occurred when the stationmaster at Mallaig spoke to the purser of the West Highland steamer, which had just berthed after a journey from the Isle of Lewis – an island famous for putting padlocks on the children's swings to prevent fun on the Sabbath.

The stationmaster shouted to the purser: 'Any goods for the Glasgow train?'

'Aye,' came the answer. 'Two jars of whisky.'

But having been told to expect whisky the stationmaster was astonished to see a large flour barrel and an earthenware jar swung aboard the train.

'But that's not a whisky jar!' he shouted.

'Oh don't worry yersel,' came the reply. 'The jar is for the Established Church minister. The other – the flour barrel – has a whisky jar hidden in it for the Free Kirk minister!'

TIME TO CHARGE

ENGLAND, 1907

The northern railway lines were always the greatest sufferers from snowfalls, but during really severe winters the southern lines could be equally bad. Only those who have been stuck in a snow drift in a train know just how terrifying that feels. The winter of 1907 brought that feeling of terror to many travellers.

Near Whitchurch in the South-West a night train was making its way through a blizzard. The snow had risen to a point a little above the wheels, and soon the train came to a standstill. The ash-pan of the engine had become choked with snow, and, with no draught, there was insufficient heat to make steam.

The guards and the fireman had to set to work to clear the thick compacted snow out of the ash-pan until steam began to be made again, but during the stoppage the carriage wheels had become clogged, so that, with the pressure in front and the increased load behind, the engine was powerless to move the train an inch.

In a brilliant if highly unusual manoeuvre to get himself out of this dreadful situation, the driver uncoupled the engine, and literally charged into the drift for two or three hundred yards and so cleared a passage. Then he returned to the train, re-coupled it to the engine and dragged it painfully along the cleared space. He then wiped out his ash-pan, uncoupled the train once more, made steam, charged headlong through the deep snow again for another quarter of a mile, returned, brought along the train, wiped his ash-pan again, charged again, and so on, until he got through the drift and resumed his laborious journey under more favourable circumstances. It was by any standards an extraordinary performance.

BY THE BOOK

ENGLAND, 1909

The railway was once famous for the size of its rulebook. Rules were designed to cover every eventuality and meticulous records were kept in every area of railway procedure. Every train that passed a signal box was logged in a big old ledger, parcels were documented and then signed for with absolute precision. And, when it came to railway discipline, procedures were equally rigorous. Even the lowliest railway employee could file a complaint and, provided it was done properly, it had to be treated with the utmost seriousness.

One incident, recorded in great detail in an old ledger, led to a highly amusing exchange between a stationmaster and his chief superintendent. The stationmaster had what he thought was a serious grievance about the extent of his duties and the inadequacy of his remuneration. He tried to find a solution locally but failed and therefore took it to headquarters.

Calling on the chief superintendent, he gave him a long-winded account of his troubles. He had completely exhausted the chief's patience by the time he commenced again going over the whole ground, and the superintendent politely told him he could do nothing in the matter. This failed to satisfy the aggrieved party, who began the whole story for a third time, with more detail and embellishments. The result was that he was ordered out of the office.

Still obsessed by a sense of injustice and dissatisfied with railway superintendents, the stationmaster by some means got access to the sanctum of the general manager, who, having heard something of his complaint, asked him why he had not gone to his superintendent.

'I've already been to him, sir,' was the reply. 'And he told me to go to the devil. So here I am.'

FOILED BY HIS OWN CARD

GERMANY, 1910

General Budde, who was Minister of Railways in Germany in the early 1900s, was never more happy than when personally looking after the perfect fulfilment of all the rules pertaining to train timetables, engine working and passenger behaviour. He was the epitome of Teutonic precision and punctuality.

The general knew that when he was out and about on his official duties his officials would invariably put on a good show for him, so on several occasions he travelled incognito on his own railway just to make sure things were being run exactly as they should be.

He once made a trip dressed in disguise to Hamburg. Halfway there, the train stopped at a small country station and a big, red-faced farmer entered his compartment, and at once proceeded to light an enormous and very smelly cigar. Though slightly concerned at the ferocious look of the farmer, the general had to speak up because smoking was not allowed on the train. As politely as possible the general pointed out that the rules of the road prohibited anyone from smoking in a compartment without the consent of the other occupants. The smoker did not seem to understand, and continued to exhale fumes like a small volcano.

Upon finishing his first cigar he immediately lit another. The general, by this time thoroughly vexed, said: 'I am well acquainted with the rules of the road, because I am the Minister of Railways.' At the same time he handed his card to the smoker. The farmer glanced at the card with an indifferent air and stuck it in his pocket without a word and without ceasing for an instant to exhale enormous puffs of smoke.

When the train finally reached its destination the farmer got out. He still hadn't said a single word. The general by this time was overcome with anger. Calling one of the station officials, he told him to go to the farmer and get his name and address, as he intended to have him arrested.

Asked his name, the smoker of the big smelly cigars pulled from his pocket a card – that of the general – and handed it to his questioner. The stationmaster glanced at the card and immediately bowed, stood to attention and produced a remarkably crisp military salute. Afterwards, returning to the 'real' general, he said: 'I believe my dear sir, that you would do well not to insist about that man breaking the rules of the road. You couldn't arrest him, anyhow, seeing as he is the Minister of Railways himself.'

The general did not insist.

MIND THE STEERING

ENGLAND, 1910

For many people during the middle decades of the nineteenth century rail travel was quite simply a dangerous enterprise. Ordinary people still clung to bizarre beliefs about rail travel – that high-speed travel damaged one's kidneys, or made the blood rush to the head or caused baldness and premature ageing. In remote country districts, particularly in Scotland, elderly people who'd lived in the same small area all their lives refused absolutely even to believe in the existence of a machine that could carry hundreds of people at 50 miles per hour, much as country people in remote parts of the world probably still refuse to believe that men have landed on the moon.

But even among those who ought to have known better, there were extraordinary and sometimes hilarious levels of ignorance. A journalist writing in *The Times* at the end of the Edwardian era described a long train journey he'd undertaken on behalf of his paper. He'd been asked to describe what it was like to be on a train that was attempting to break a speed record and the railway company, anxious to get as much publicity as possible for their high-speed services, agreed to allow the journalist to travel on the footplate.

The journey started sedately enough on the straight run out of King's Cross station and the journalist later wrote that he'd been impressed by the extraordinary acceleration of which the great fire-breathing monster was capable. But the driver and fireman knew that something was wrong when on each occasion that the

269

train approached a tunnel the journalist became incredibly agitated, darting from one side of the footplate to the other, shouting 'Be careful! You're going to miss!' and getting in the way of driver and fireman.

After several tunnels he looked so white with obvious panic that the footplate men thought they might have to make an unscheduled stop to let him off. But the crisis passed and they reached their destination. The journalist climbed down from the cab and tottered off along the platform looking decidedly shell-shocked.

When his article appeared several weeks later the explanation for his bizarre behaviour became clear.

As he described the journey, the journalist was full of praise for the extraordinary way the driver managed to steer the train into the tiny black holes (he meant the tunnel entrances) that appeared in the distance now and then. 'What's more,' continued the writer, 'I could not see how the driver did it. Certainly he looked up ahead continually but no movement of his arms revealed the means by which he steered that massive engine with all its attendant coaches into the tunnels with only a foot or two space to spare on either side!'

MR LEAROYD'S RECORD

ENGLAND, 1910

A whim for attempting novel things and a penchant for touring led Mr J Ingham Learoyd, a well-known Halifax businessman, to test the possibility of travelling 1,000 miles on a British railway in a single day. His first plan was to attempt the feat by zig-zagging across England, but the timetables made this impossible and the idea of hiring special trains was dismissed on the grounds of expense. The only way to do it – despite the bizarre pointlessness of the proceeding – was to travel long distances to and fro on one system. Mr Ingham Learoyd chose the Midland.

Starting from London's St Pancras station at midnight one Monday, Mr Learoyd journeyed to Leeds, reaching that city at 4.30am. In seven minutes he began the return journey, getting back to St Pancras at 8.15am, having so far accounted for 391 miles in 488 minutes. Next, boarding the 9.30 North express again at St Pancras, he was rushed to Carlisle, some 381 miles away, arriving there at 3.50, or in 380 minutes, and leaving only an 8-minute margin before he had to be seated in a return train for London, due at 10:25.

Punctuality was so assured in those far-off days that the entire programme, fine as the margins were, was carried through as planned: 1,008 miles were travelled in, as nearly as possible, 1,260 minutes or 180 minutes inside the specified time. Mr Learoyd carried a certificate with three of his portraits for identification purposes, and at each terminal by pre-arrangement, a railway official stamped specially prepared documentation.

The intrepid traveller said that for two years he had been contemplating his strange journey and that during that time he had studied the timetables so intensively that he knew them off by heart. Learoyd actually spent just 21 hours travelling, and the distance he covered worked out an average of 48 miles per hour.

SPLENDID NAVVIES

ENGLAND, 1910

To a very large extent it was the Irish who built the railway system that we still use today. The huge earthworks involved in creating cuttings and embankments, in laying track and ballast represent the life's work of countless thousands of anonymous labourers from remote rural hamlets and villages in Ireland. But then the Irish also worked in their thousands for the railways, once the tracks were laid and the whole vast infrastructure in place. They became drivers, firemen, porters and managers. And, like the Irish everywhere, they were famous for their skill with words; and none more so than the porters who worked in the great stations in Liverpool, Birmingham and London.

But the porter's lot was not generally a happy one – he worked long hours for little pay and often had to put up with the insolence of the travelling public whose rudeness it was said often increased in proportion to their wealth and status.

A porter from New Ross in Wexford was famous for his ability to tell rude passengers what he thought of them without having to resort to rudeness himself. His colleagues used to say that when he put someone in their place the best thing about it was that the passenger didn't realise what had happened until he or she was 50 miles into their journey.

An angry traveller once shouted: 'What is the good of having a timetable if your trains are always late?'

The porter scratched his head and replied: 'And how would you know the trains were late if we didn't give you a timetable?'

273

A classic example of the Irishman's wit came when a very grand lady began shouting and beckoning to him while he was trying to deal with another passenger. She refused to wait and continued shouting even while it was obvious that the porter could not easily disengage himself without being very rude. However, at last he was able to deal with the grand lady.

'Porter, porter!' she shouted crossly, 'Come here at once.'

'How can I help?' said the porter.

'I've lost my luggage!' said the grand lady.

'For what might ye be wanting a porter then?' came the reply.

Only rarely did the porter show that he really was angry but once, on a summer morning in 1910, the shouting and abuse became too much and the witty porter rose majestically to the challenge – he told the passenger where, as it were, to get off. The porter had been standing on the platform just as a train began to pull away when what he later described as a 'very snooty head' appeared at a window and began shouting at him.

'You idiot!' shouted the snooty head. 'Why didn't you put my luggage in as I told you?'

'Your luggage is not such a fool as you, madam – you're on the wrong train!'

'Is this train punctual?' he was asked by a passenger on another occasion.

'Yes madam,' he replied, 'it is generally a quarter of an hour late to the minute!'

In all his long career only one man got the better of him. He once ran up to a bishop, who was surrounded by various boxes and suitcases and said:

'How many articles, my Lord?'

'Thirty-nine,' came the prelate's reply.

SLIGHT MISUNDERSTANDING

ENGLAND, 1911

A bishop spent an hour trying to locate the stationmaster at Paddington in order to have a porter sacked. The bishop was furious because he thought the porter had deliberately insulted him. It was only when the circumstances had been explained to the stationmaster that the bishop – famously tetchy and convinced of his own importance – realised that he had made a complete fool of himself.

The story begins with the system for dealing with luggage at Paddington. In the early days it was the practice for luggage coming by train to be carried to a long bench overhung by the letters of the alphabet. To claim his luggage Mr Smith would, for example, go to the letter S, Mr Brown to the letter B and so on.

When the bishop, a little the worse for drink, arrived at the station he found a porter and – completely ignorant of the Paddington method for sorting luggage – asked where he should go to find his bags.

'What is your name?' said the porter.

'Llewellyn,' said the bishop.

'Go to L,' said the porter.

The bishop's face turned red and without a word he set off in search of the stationmaster.

SIGNING THE PEACE

FRANCE, 1918

Over the past 150 years and more, children have no doubt occasionally been conceived in railway carriages. Women have given birth on trains and, sadly, the elderly have been known to depart this world while on a journey on the iron road. Many other momentous events have taken place on trains from murders to christenings, seances to marriages. But perhaps the most momentous event ever recorded in a railway carriage occurred in 1918.

The carriage still exists and to this day it stands on a sector of what was the Western Front during the First World War. Long removed from active service, the carriage is, in appearance, just an ordinary carriage, typical of the design used by the French Railway Service in the years up to and after the Great War, but within it was signed the Armistice that stilled the millions of guns and rifles that for more than four years had levied their toll of death over a 1,000-mile front.

Few places have the significance of this simple carriage, where the document was signed that brought peace to a grief-stricken Europe.

RUDE AWAKENING

CANADA, 1919

The Canadian Pacific Line's officers had a delightful trip from Winnipeg to attend the officers' meeting and banquet held in Montreal in the early part of 1919. A large western delegation was aboard, and nobody ever thought of retiring to bed until the milkmen were on their rounds in the grey mornings.

On the morning on which they reached Montreal they went to bed at about three o'clock. The train was scheduled to arrive at its destination at six, and the intention of the officers was to sleep until eight or nine. But Jim Woodman, the Terminal Superintendent, had decreed otherwise, as he considered the occasion should be suitably honoured by giving the western officers a royal welcome. As soon, therefore, as the train came to rest on No.2 track, a switch engine meandered down the adjoining track at a slow pace, slow even for an engine of that type, and at every rail-length, exploded a detonator, known in railway parlance as a torpedo or a fog-signal.

The noise of the explosions was deafening, and the reverberations in the great train shed were simply terrifying. Finally the engine reached the end of the track and the din ceased, but immediately there rose on the morning air strains of music from two large and very noisy hurdy-gurdies, operated by a couple of early rising Italians specially employed for the occasion. The occupants of the carriages desperately trying to sleep after their night of carousing had first been terrified by the apparent explosions and gunfire as the detonators went off and were now deafened by the wild cacophony of these strange musical instruments. One later said that in his half-asleep state it was like the worst nightmare he could imagine.

By this time most of the passengers on the train were awake and they were throwing everything they could lay their hands on out the windows in an attempt to stop the deafening roar of the music. The poor Italians found themselves deluged by a rain of plates and cups, bits of old food, packages, bars of soap, knives and forks. They also shouted and swore from the windows to such an extent that the police had to be called to prevent the situation getting out of hand. The Italians had been told that on no account were they to stop playing or they would not be paid. So they planted themselves, one on either side of the Vice President's carriage, which was filled with dignitaries and VIPs. The Italians were deaf to imprecations, threats and bribes, and peace was only restored when the train was moved up the line and beyond the reach of the musicians.

POMP AND CIRCUMSTANCE

ENGLAND, 1923

Members of parliament and other notables spend their lives climbing the greasy pole of advancement and tend to take themselves very seriously indeed, to believe that the world revolves around them and is as fascinated by their lives as they are themselves. Very occasionally ordinary mortals get the chance to see the great brought low or are at least reminded that they are not quite as important under all circumstances as they think they are.

A particularly arrogant Tory candidate for a seat in the English Midlands had just come top of the poll. He was on the one hand overjoyed because his majority had been far bigger than he'd expected and on the other embarrassingly puffed up with pride and a sense of his own importance.

He had arrived at the station with his entourage to take the train to London and waved at anyone who even vaguely looked in his direction. Most of those he passed in fact hadn't a clue who he was. He reached the platform and when the London train pulled in he climbed aboard. When he entered his compartment a small man in the far corner stood up. Looking in his direction, the great man waved his hand and said condescendingly:

'Good morning, good morning. Pray sit down, that really is quite unnecessary.'

'Why the devil should I sit down?' came the reply, 'I'm getting out here!'

279

TICKET TRICKS

ENGLAND, 1924

The tricks used by the travelling public to reduce the costs of a journey haven't changed much in over 150 years of railway travel. Twenty-year-olds trying to pass themselves off as children in order to obtain half-fare tickets, have always been the bane of the ticket inspector's life. Likewise the traveller who buys a standard-class ticket and then – when he or she thinks no one is about – sneaks into a first-class compartment.

When, as is almost inevitable, these tricksters are caught, most have the sense to keep their heads down, mumble an apology and pay the proper fare or quickly move to second class. One or two rather more witty individuals have stuck up for themselves and in the process they have become railway legends.

A traveller on the London and North Eastern Railway earned his place in the pantheon of railway wits after being caught with a second-class ticket in a first-class compartment. When he was confronted by the ticket inspector the following exchange took place:

Inspector: 'You have no call to be in here. You haven't got a first-class ticket.'

Traveller: 'No. I haven't.'

Inspector: 'Well come out; this isn't a second-class carriage.'

Traveller (astonished): 'Isn't it? I thought it was by the look of the passengers in there!'

TRAIN ROBBERS MEET THEIR MATCH

ENGLAND, 1925

One would think that strange rail journeys would be exclusively associated with drivers, guards and passengers and not with the signalman in his often lonely and isolated box. But of course there are exceptions to every rule and at least one signalman got mixed up in a remarkable adventure.

It all began when the railway authorities got wind of a plan to hold up and rob a train that was conveying boxes of gold to Southampton for shipment to America. The secret of the shipment had somehow leaked out, and half a dozen desperate characters, ex-jailbirds, apparently decided that the gold had better stay in England and with them.

The first part of their plan to steal the gold involved overpowering an elderly signalman at a lonely countryside place, afterwards working the signals themselves. They proposed to bring the gold train to a standstill, tie up the driver and the guard, and carry away the spoil by car.

Perhaps the plan was inspired by something the criminals had seen on the cinema screen. They thought their plan was foolproof but then fate took a hand in events. The old signalman, who was to have been overpowered and captured, was taken ill with a serious bout of flu and a younger man came to do the job for a time. He was a strong man, too, and an amateur boxer who could have been a professional but for the fact that he loved his job on the railways. When the train robbers climbed the steps of his box in the dead of night, little did they suspect what awaited them.

The first robber crept through the door, made a rush at the signalman in the half light and was knocked clean unconscious by a perfectly executed right hook. The signalman reached the door of his box and the next man came at him up the stairs. Train robber number two was knocked flying. From then on the signalman knocked them down the steps of the signal box as fast as they came up, and the gold train ran by in safety while they were counting their bruises. Afterwards the police rounded up the lot of them and, though covered as they were in fresh cuts and bruises, there were few problems identifying them!

HOPELESS VOLUNTEER

ENGLAND, 1926

During the General Strike, volunteer firemen, drivers, porters and guards were taken on and in general they made a thoroughly bad job of running those industries that had come to a halt as the result of the walkout. On the railway most of the volunteers were from well-off backgrounds and they had no experience of hard manual work of any kind. Many were lucky enough to have private incomes as they were, to be frank, fit for no kind of employment. The railway was particularly badly afflicted with this kind of volunteer, but their presence led to one or two amusing incidents. A good example occurred on a suburban train that left London and then had a long steep climb. It made it to the top of the incline by the narrowest of margins and the volunteer guard ran to the front of the train to discuss their narrow escape with the driver.

'My word,' said the driver, as the volunteer guard reached the footplate, 'I never thought we'd make the top of that hill.'

'Yes,' said the volunteer guard, 'and you have me to thank for the fact that we didn't run backwards. Thank goodness I screwed the brake down hard!'

RUNAWAY CHILD

ENGLAND, 1926

Train spotters will always be with us. Despite the mockery to which they are so frequently subjected, generation after generation of list-making train enthusiasts have spent their lives not travelling by train but watching trains in the hope that they may finally spot every locomotive on a particular network or region.

In the days of steam there was an element of romance to the train spotter's passion, but with diesel and electric trains it is all but impossible for the outsider to understand what makes a grown man stand all day at the end of a draughty platform jotting down numbers.

Travelling by train is another matter altogether and many of those who find train spotting incomprehensible would be the first to opt for a life of habitual train travel. Which is perhaps why it is easy to sympathise with the extraordinary child who spent two years (when he should have been at school) travelling illegally all over Britain by train.

Eight-year-old Luke Westall disappeared in the autumn of 1926 from the little Northamptonshire village where his family had lived for generations.

At first it looked like a classic and terrible case of abduction. Luke left one sunny morning to walk to the village school less than half a mile away – a journey he had made on his own many times before – but he never arrived. Police searched high and low for weeks but not a trace of the boy was found. He became just another statistic at a time when it was estimated that more than twenty thousand youngsters disappeared without trace each year.

Nearly two years after Luke vanished a very dirty and bedraggled boy was taken off the Edinburgh train at King's Cross and led across to a disused office. A sharp-eyed guard had spotted the boy and was sure he'd seen him at least twice in recent weeks and each time without an accompanying adult.

As the guard later explained he was convinced there was something odd about the boy because his clothes seemed too small for him and almost shiny with age, yet he was wearing what looked like the tattered remnants of a school uniform.

The guard asked the boy to wait in the office while he tried to find the stationmaster. By the time he returned the boy had vanished, but an alert for was issued and over the next few months sightings of him – or at least of a boy answering his description – were frequent. On several occasions the boy was nearly caught but each time he managed to slip away only to be seen a day or two later on another train.

The boy's ability to evade capture was remarkable, but his mother later said he had always been 'a delightful but mischievous little blighter' who had many times tried to persuade his well-behaved sister Emma to take part in his schemes and pranks. When he was finally caught, he'd been on the run for nearly two and a half years. At first he refused to say anything about his time away from home, refusing even to confirm or deny that he'd been abducted, but within a few days his curious reluctance to speak seemed to melt away and he told his tale.

On the morning he left home he decided, on a whim, not to go to school and set off instead for the nearest town where he caught the train to Peterborough. As he was small it was easy, he said, to sneak through the barrier and on to the main London train. During the journey and all those journeys that were to follow, he moved seats regularly and tried to give the impression that he'd wandered away from his parents in order to look around the train.

He said that he had enjoyed that first journey so much that when the train reached London he simply found out the time of the next train to the north and got on it, reaching Edinburgh the next day. Over the coming months he travelled continually up and down the main east coast line, taking odd detours as the fancy took him and even sneaking on to the sleeper to Inverness now and then. All this time he lived on discarded sandwiches, apples and anything he could scavenge. He slept rough at stations or in the fields near country stations, but with every journey his desire to travel increased and he began to travel more widely, up the west coast and into Scotland and Wales. He never once felt homesick or worried about his future and, despite the fact that he'd been happy at home, he never once – or so he said – missed his parents. But he was devoted to his sister and had missed her terribly, worrying that, during his absence, she might be taken away by a stranger.

His family and the authorities found it hard to believe that a young child had been able to travel for so long without being apprehended and some doubted little Luke's story. It seemed incredible that two years could pass before anyone noticed this continuously travelling child. The oddest part of the story, however, is that once he'd returned to his home Luke stayed put; he never so much as mentioned trains again.

STRANGE PACKAGE

ENGLAND, 1926

The officers of the Midland Railway depot in Liverpool were asked to go down to the platform where a strange package from the South of France had just arrived on the 8.35 express. The package was destined to be sent on to the USA, but there was something highly suspicious about it. The guard on the train had raised the alarm after noticing a strange smell.

The increasingly large group of railway officials had the package, which was rather large, carried to the railway post office. There they debated whether or not they should open it. Under normal circumstances any package entrusted to the railway was treated with the utmost discretion and opening a packet without permission was something contemplated only in extreme circumstances. But the longer they looked at the package the more worried they became. A decision was made to open the crate. When this was done it was found to contain a beautifully ornamented coffin containing the embalmed body of an American, fully dressed and complete with cowboy hat, guns, belt and boots.

Under the rules of parcel carrying that existed in the nineteenth century bodies were not permitted to be posted around the world. There was nothing for it but to impound the coffin and its cowboy. The crate was sealed up again and left in the lost property office while officials contacted the Chicago station that was its destination. In Chicago, advertisements were taken out to try to trace the owners of the crate, but two years later no one had come forward and the embalmed cowboy's identity remained a mystery.

After that, all efforts to trace the owners of the crate or relatives of the dead American ceased and the crate remained at Liverpool for more than twenty years. Most of those who'd stood around examining the coffin when it was first discovered were long dead or retired by the time an official checking the old ledgers spotted an entry for the coffin and noted too that the crate had never been collected. He took down the reference number that indicated where the crate was stored but when he went to check it was still there, not a trace could be found. And it has not been seen since.

CHEESE SMUGGLER

AMERICA 1927

During a strike in an American city in the 1920s it was found necessary to place an embargo on all inbound freight and express shipments for a short period. A grocer who was mightily put out by this, and being absolutely out of Limburger cheese, made an extremely attractive offer for a large consignment of his favourite cheese on the condition that it would reach its destination within four days from the time the order was accepted.

A manufacturer located about two hundred miles distant undertook to fulfil the order, but finding that it could not be shipped by rail because of the strike, he bought a coffin, in which he placed the cheese, and screwing the lid down securely, he bought a ticket for himself and one for a corpse and started off with his unsavoury consignment.

Judging by the malodorousness of the Limburger, it was of a superior quality. The cheese was so strong, in fact, that the train baggageman spent most of the time on the trip with his head thrust out through the carriage door. Arriving at his destination the 'mourner' appeared on the station platform opposite the carriage door wearing black crepe on his hat and looking forlorn and heartbroken.

After transferring the 'corpse' to a truck the baggageman stepped down to the platform and, sidling up to the 'mourner', said in a sympathetic voice, 'Your father?'

'No, he was my brother,' was the sad reply.

'Well,' said the baggageman, 'I sympathise deeply with you, but it may be some slight comfort for you to know that – judging by the smell – he is most definitely not in a trance!'

289

MYSTERY CHILDREN

ENGLAND, 1928

Early one misty October morning a Bristol-bound freight train, a passenger train from Birmingham and an empty fifty-wagon train collided near the village of Charfield, at that time still in Gloucestershire. Dozens of people were killed, including two children. A terrible tragedy by any standards, but also the beginning of one of the greatest of unsolved mysteries, for the two children who died have never been identified.

The railway company insisted the two children had not been on the train and that the two small bodies actually belonged to two strays who'd been sheltering under the railway bridge at the time of the crash. But the driver of the passenger train survived the crash and spoke up. He explained how he had waved to the two well-dressed children when they boarded the train at New Street, Birmingham. He had noticed them – the girl aged about eight, the boy eleven – because they were unaccompanied and without luggage.

Legend has it that for years after the crash an elderly woman in black, driven by a chauffeur, visited the grave at Charfield where ten victims of the crash (including the children) are buried. After the war, she ceased to come and there is no evidence anyway that her visits were not to remember one of the other victims.

As each year passes there is less chance of identifying the children and their story remains one of the greatest of all railway mysteries.

INTO THE BLIZZARD

TURKEY, 1929

It was a cold January evening when the *Orient Express* left Paris for Venice. A number of English aristocrats were aboard the train, including the King's bag carrier, one Major Custance. Hardly had the train left the station than it began to be buffeted by terrifying gusts of wind. Heavy snow was driven so hard against the train that the windows were soon covered with a layer three inches thick. The passengers grew nervous. The wind howled and the whole train was rocked from side to side as the blasts of wind grew ever more violent.

It was the worst storm in living memory. Northern seas were turning to ice, hundreds of villages and towns across Europe had ground to a halt; smaller, more remote communities would be completely cut off for weeks. Temperatures were so low that frost-bite afflicted thousands in parts of the world where it was previously unheard of. Temperatures regularly touched 35 degrees below freezing.

But bad weather was not going to stop Europe's most prestigious rail service. When the *Orient Express* reached Venice, urgent consultations were held, but despite the appalling weather the luxury train was given the all-clear for Vienna. The truth is that the officials who made the decision allowed their concern for the reputation of the train to cloud their judgement.

As the train left the station at Vienna it was clear that both passengers and railway officials were nervous. The night wore on and with dawn came a curious air of normality; despite the dreadful conditions just outside the carriages the usual magnificent breakfast was served in the dining car. The train headed towards the Tyrol and the blizzard worsened.

More by luck than judgement they reached Vienna where they were told that snow ploughs had been working on the line ahead of them. It was that piece of information more than any other that persuaded them to continue. By a miracle they reached Budapest. The Danube was frozen solid to a depth of perhaps two feet. Despite the worst reports so far – that the line was blocked in Romania by huge snow drifts – the train was given the all-clear. It was almost as if a disastrous fatalism had infected everyone.

A few hours after leaving Budapest, the express had to slow to a snail's pace simply to ensure that the ferocious winds didn't blow it off the tracks. Even at a crawl the poor fireman had to work flat out to keep the engine running at all. Across Bulgaria the weather became even more atrocious, with massive blankets of snow building up on the top and sides of the train. Then the fuel froze along with the heating pipes. As they crossed into Turkey they hit snow drifts on the line itself – each time the driver ran into one he reversed along the track and, as it were, took a run at the drift, each time managing to break through, but at last even the skill and courage of the driver could do no more against the full horror of the storm and, a few miles from the village of Corlu, a massive 25-foot-high drift of hard compacted snow stopped them dead. Once the train had stopped it didn't take long for pretty much everything to freeze.

First the cylinder pipes froze (which meant there was a serious risk of an explosion) and then the reversing gear stuck fast. The snow around them was twice the height of the train and their narrow valley was rapidly being filled in. Their only chance was to dig a way out through the massive drift ahead of them: if they failed the whole train would soon be buried. Walking was impossible and the telegraph lines were down so there was no way to summon help. Guard, steward, driver and fireman discussed their predicament and decided they had enough food for two days. The boiler was still supplying some heat to the carriages, but for how much longer?

Panic gripped the passengers, many of whom (in those far-off days when the well-to-do had servants) had never in their lives had to fend for themselves or do anything practical. With food and water suddenly rationed they began to bicker and quarrel. A night and a day passed and the train sank steadily further into the snow. The passengers then realised that help was not going to come in time and they would have to fend for themselves.

They were asked by the driver and Major Custance, who had taken charge, to volunteer to help clear the snow. Those who volunteered, which was pretty much everyone, were split into two groups, each group digging for just 15 minutes before retreating to their carriages to warm up. Any longer and exhaustion and frostbite would quickly set in. But, even alternating like this, the two groups found it difficult to make any progress.

They began to think that there was little hope of digging themselves out, so the head chef and one of the waiters set off on foot for the nearest village which, according to the one map they were able to find in one of the passenger's luggage, was just three miles away. When the two men reached the village after walking laboriously for several hours they were greeted by a group of heavily armed, wild-looking men who at first refused to help in any way. The situation was made worse by the fact that the two men from the train hadn't a clue what sort of bizarre dialect these wild-looking men spoke.

At last they were able to buy a few chickens and some bread. No practical offers of help were forthcoming so the men returned to the train.

The following night the passengers were so cold, hungry and depressed that one of them, a young singer, tried to cut her wrists. The chef and several waiters set off for the village again the next morning and came back with more food but only after narrowly escaping an attack by wolves on the return journey. But several passengers were now in a bad way, in addition to the singer who had been bandaged and sedated, but was at least still alive.

Food was now strictly rationed and, as the days passed, the passengers and crew grew more listless. It took six full days for the authorities finally to reach the stranded train. The rescue party – a large contingent of Turkish soldiers – reached them behind snowploughs and a spare engine. The stranded train was slowly hauled to Constantinople.

The whole incident made headlines all over the world. All the passengers recovered from their ordeal and the woman who'd tried to slit her wrists – Paula von Werner – changed her act and began to call herself The Singing Heroine of the Orient Express. She became a sensation and sang all over Europe to packed houses. She later said that without the incident on the *Orient Express* her career never would have taken off.

MISSING MUMMY

ENGLAND, 1930

It's almost impossible to believe now but in the late nineteenth century tens of thousands of mummified cats and other mummified animals plundered from Egyptian tombs were shipped by train and boat to Liverpool, ground down and then sold to farmers in the north-west of England to be used as fertiliser.

But with the discovery of Tutankhamen's tomb in 1929 Egyptology was suddenly taken far more seriously. The quality of the artefacts discovered was extraordinary and their design had an enormous influence on culture and art generally and more specifically on the Art Deco movement of the twenties and thirties. Mummies – at least of humans – suddenly became valuable commodities and they were transported from the Valley of the Kings to museums and collectors all over the world. Anyone with any pretensions to wealth and taste wanted a mummy in their art collection, which meant prices soared and the black market trade flourished.

One particularly interesting and valuable mummy was discovered and sold to a wealthy collector in the North of England. It consisted of a beautifully carved stone sarcophagus containing a magnificently decorated wooden casket and, inside that, the mummified remains of a princess. Every inch of the wooden casket was covered with hieroglyphics; the portrait of the deceased on the head of the casket was particularly fine and the bandages that enclosed the mummy were still decorated with the beads and other pieces of jewellery that had lain undisturbed for more than three thousand years.

But how was this priceless antiquity to be brought safely to Cheshire? The answer was first by rail to the port of Alexandria and then by ship to Liverpool. From there the train would have to carry the princess to the grand house in Cheshire that was to be her new home.

All went well on the first two stages of the journey and it was only when the North Western Railway Company took charge that things began to go wrong. In its big wooden crate, the stone sarcophagus and its contents weighed several tons and, when the time came for it to be loaded into the train on the docks, it took more than a dozen porters to manoeuvre the thing into the specially commissioned freight wagon in which it was to be transported. All went well and the train was soon speeding away from the smoky city out into the countryside.

By the time the train had stopped at the first of three scheduled stops something quite extraordinary had happened. The freight wagon was no longer attached to the train – it had vanished. No one had seen it go and enquiries up and down the line over the next few days revealed absolutely nothing about its whereabouts. There were two single branch lines it could have taken – though how anyone could have removed it from the train, changed the points and manoeuvred the wagon off down a different line baffled police and railway investigators.

Months passed and nothing was heard of the mummy. Then eight months after the incident a schoolboy playing in fields at the edge of one of the branch lines discovered the badly damaged freight wagon. It had been cleverly concealed under masses of brushwood, leaves and branches in thick woodland at the bottom of the railway embankment. All traces of its derailment from the line above and down through the trees had been obliterated. The point on the line where the wagon had been deliberately derailed was just a few hundred yards from the junction with the main line and, once it had been discovered, it seemed extraordinary that it hadn't been spotted before.

This was all long before police work had the benefit of forensic science, so the examination of the freight wagon and surrounding area was at best cursory. Nothing of any significance was found but one thing was clear – the valuable mummy, its casket and the sarcophagus were long gone. But how on earth had such a large, heavy object been carried across the field, presumably to the nearest road, and then carted away without anything being seen?

Over the next two years the mummy's owner received reports that it had been spotted in various museums around the world but, when he made enquiries, it always turned out to be a different mummy. Trying to track down his lost mummy became something of a crusade for the wealthy aristocrat. He spent a great deal of money on private detectives who travelled Europe checking museums and private collections. He took to travelling the country – by train of course – and hung around left luggage offices in the vain hope that his long-lost prize possession would somehow materialise. It never did and the old man died without ever recovering his property.

In a curious twist there were reports twenty years after the old man died that a stone coffin covered with strange writing was found half buried in a field 200 miles from the place where the mummy originally disappeared. In a curious twist of fate, the stone coffin was found just a few yards from a railway line, but, by the time anyone realised that it was a thing of some value, it had been broken up by workmen and dispersed.

WALKING ON AIR

ENGLAND, 1933

However good the regulations and however well carriages and locomotives are looked after, accidents will always happen on the railway. It is difficult now to know whether travelling by train was once far safer than it is now. That's the popular view, but it is difficult to find evidence to prove it. Electronic control systems are probably more reliable than the old systems, but that advantage may well be outweighed by the fact that in the days of steam there were far more staff keeping an eye on things.

Most accidents, of course, involve trains colliding with each other or passengers falling on the track. Unlike passengers, railway staff have a sixth sense about what to do and what not to do so they rarely get into trouble, but one conductor had an extraordinary escape on a journey in 1933 from London to York. His train was approaching Grantham at nearly 70 miles per hour and the conductor was walking along the corridors away from the engine as the train entered Peascliffe Tunnel. Walking from one coach into the next in the dark he found he was walking on air. The partition had not been connected to the vestibule connection of the last coach.

Incredibly, the conductor was unhurt despite tumbling on to the hard ballast at such speed. A search party sent back from Grantham to look for him found him making his way towards the town along the side of the tracks. He was a little dusty and shaken but otherwise none the worse for his ordeal.

STOP THE TRAIN

SCOTLAND, 1935

The North of Scotland Railway runs through some of Europe's most remote countryside. Until recently there were steep-sided valleys here where isolated farmers could not even receive radio or TV signals. But, despite the remoteness of the countryside, the enthusiastic railway builders had allowed for a station wherever they thought there might be the least interest in occasional travel. This meant there were lots of stations in the middle of nowhere.

To reduce the huge costs of stopping the trains at these outposts regularly, a rule was established that the trains would slow down as they ran through the stations and stop only if a passenger was there on the platform and trying to flag the train down. This worked well in most areas, but one or two of the older farmers didn't quite grasp the principle of the thing and for years railway staff dined out on the story of old McMurdo who flagged down one of the few busy trains early one evening. The engine driver knew McMurdo and was astonished to see him waving the train down – McMurdo was famous for never travelling anywhere whatever the circumstances.

But he was certainly waving and the rules stated that if a passenger wanted the train then the train had to stop. The driver applied the brakes and the train came to a halt. The driver leaned out of the cab and shouted back along the platform to McMurdo.

'Where are you going this time of night, Davie?'

'Oh, I'm not getting on,' said Davie McMurdo, 'I just wanted to tell you my wife will be getting on in the morning!'

THE JOURNEY THAT NEVER WAS

ENGLAND, 1936

Prejudice against the railway lasted well into the twentieth century. In a few remote parts of Britain men and women who'd been young when the railway first came to their districts in the 1860s and 1870s grew up with a loathing for the new method of transport that no amount of familiarity would dispel.

One elderly Westmoreland farmer travelled once on the train when he was in his twenties and was terrified by the experience: 'I knew immediately this noise and chaos and terror meant no good to the future of mankind!' He is reported to have vowed not only never to travel again by train but also to forbid any member of his family ever to travel by train.

The old man had no children but late in his long life (when he was in his eighties, in fact) he developed a fondness for a great nephew who was in his early teens. He told the young man's parents that he would make the boy his heir – and he had amassed a significant fortune – but only on condition that the young man sign a legal contract agreeing that he would never travel on 'that ungodly iron road that has been the curse of our age'.

Despite the bizarre nature of the request the young man and his parents agreed that for the sake of the legacy he should sign, which he duly did in 1936, in front of the old man, a lawyer and several witnesses. And he was as good as his word – by all accounts he simply moved into the old man's farmhouse when the old man finally died and he never broke his word. He died in the 1960s having never, so far as anyone could tell, travelled by train. An example perhaps of the most extraordinary train journey that never happened!

HIGH-SPEED RECORD

ENGLAND, 1937

Within a few decades of the invention of the locomotive, trains were running at extraordinarily fast speeds because technical development – as in so many areas – was rapid. The pressure to make trains run ever faster was largely economic; the company with the fastest trains would attract the greatest number of passengers and the greatest profits.

One way in which the early railway could show off was to run regular speed trials with prizes for the fastest runs, and the speeds those early trains achieved are extraordinary by any standards. By 1938 the Union Pacific Railroad's Mighty 80 class locomotive was able to pull a 1,000-ton passenger train on the level at just over 110 miles per hour, developing some 6,000 horse power in the cylinders in order to do so. Then the Northern Pacific Railroad ran the longest continuous run (of 1,008 miles from Minneapolis to Livingston) for coal-burning steam power – the amount of coal the train had to carry was colossal.

In 1903 an electric railcar built by the A E G Company of Germany achieved a staggering speed – a fraction under 132 mph, to produce a record that was to stand for many years. Then in 1931 an extraordinary propeller-driven vehicle, also German, managed 143 mph on the Berlin–Hamburg main line. In 1966 a similar locomotive – again propeller-driven – ran on the New York Central Railroad. Two aircraft jet engines were mounted on its roof and to the terror of the driver and spectators – who dashed away from the line as the train approached their vantage point – it reached a speed of 183.8 mph!

302

But the most extraordinary record-breaking speed was achieved by a London, Midland & Scottish Railway Coronation train from London to Crewe in June 1937. As the train descended down the famous long straight into Crewe the driver pulled out all the stops, but his bosses (who had urged him to attempt the speed record) had failed properly to calculate the length of track that would be necessary to stop a train moving downhill at over 110 mph!

When the train reached 113 mph the driver cut off the power – he'd matched the existing all-time speed record and clearly thought better than trying to add a mile or two per hour to that figure. But at the point when he shut down the power he was just two miles south of the station. He applied the brakes as hard as he could but the mass energy of the train was so huge that initially the brakes had absolutely no effect.

The terror of those on the footplate can only be imagined. Some braking effect was eventually achieved but not before the train ran through a series of cross-overs leading to the platform line, at a speed nearer 60 mph than 20 (20 was the speed those crossovers were designed to take).

Crockery crashed in the dining car, the carriages lurched dangerously, luggage flew around but, miraculously, no one was hurt as the driver brought the train to a halt only a yard or so beyond the marker at the end of the platform.

It was later discovered from marks on the tracks that the train had come within a hair's-breadth of total disaster. The marks suggested that if the train had ridden up above the rails a fraction further it would have been derailed and to this day it is a completely mystery as to why this did not, in fact, happen.

BAG MAN

ENGLAND, 1937

Getting a seat on a train can be fraught with difficulty. Other passengers will go to the most extraordinary lengths to keep an extra seat to themselves. Tactics include pretending to fall asleep stretched across two or even three seats or throwing their luggage about as if to say to other passengers 'I dare you to even suggest that my valuable luggage could possibly be put anywhere else.'

This is particularly annoying on a long journey or when the traveller with no seat has already had a difficult journey to the station. But there is a way round the problem, as a young man discovered in the 1930s. He was a regular traveller and the station staff knew and liked him as much for his ready wit as for his generous tips.

He'd just got to the station with seconds to spare before the train left. He was helped through the door of the first available carriage by a porter he knew well and, having wandered along the corridor, he entered a compartment containing a lot of luggage strewn over the seats, but with only one occupant, a young man in the corner seat.

The incoming passenger was preparing to make himself comfortable in another corner seat, but was informed that the bag, which was placed there, belonged to the young man's friend, who would be along in a minute.

The newcomer therefore stood about feeling uncomfortable and irritated. No one appeared and presently the train began very slowly to glide out of the station. Still he stood there and became all the while increasingly angry at the young man's indifference to his plight.

As the train began to pick up speed along the platform the standing passenger bent down, lifted up the offending bag and gently dropped it out of the window, remarking benignly: 'Well, your friend won't want to lose both his train and his bag!'

ALWAYS LATE

ENGLAND, 1937

The Eastern Counties Railway was for decades a byword for late trains – so much so that even when things improved dramatically the jokes continued. Typical of these was the *Punch* magazine jibe about a young man who was seen to go to the Shoreditch terminus of the Eastern Counties Railway and buy a ticket for Cambridge. 'No motive has been ascribed for this exceedingly rash act,' comments the magazine.

Another favourite joke concerned the passenger who travelled on the same morning train for 25 years. Not once had it been on time. Then, a few days before the man was due to retire from his job and cease making his daily journey, the train arrived bang on time.

The traveller was so delighted that he went up to the footplate to congratulate the driver and offer him a cigar. The driver wistfully replied that he could not take the cigar.

'Why on earth not?' said the passenger.

'I should have been here at this time yesterday,' came the reply.

But the jokes were often based on real incidents and none better illustrates the problems with the region's trains than the incident involving the guard who was so fed up with complaints about slow trains and late trains and trains that simply didn't appear at all that he developed a fierce and sarcastic personality.

His reputation soared when one morning a woman leaned out of the window of a particularly slow train and shouted at the guard: 'Can't you go any faster?'

'Well perhaps I could ma'am,' said the guard, 'but it's my job to stay with the train!'

BEECHAM'S HOWLERS

ENGLAND, 1938

The great conductor and eccentric Sir Thomas Beecham was travelling in a non-smoking compartment on a train belonging to the Great Western Railway. A lady entered the compartment and lit a cigarette, saying, 'I'm sure you won't object if I smoke.'

'Not at all,' replied Beecham, 'provided that you don't object if I'm sick.'

'I don't think you know who I am,' the lady haughtily pointed out. 'I'm one of the directors' wives.'

'Madam,' said Beecham, 'if you were the director's only wife I should still be sick.'

UNBEATEN RECORD

ENGLAND, 1938

On 3 July 1938 a world speed record for a steam train was set on the East Coast Edinburgh to London line. What was most remarkable about this record breaking run – which reached 126 mph on the Stoke Summit between London and York – is that it has never to this day been beaten.

The engine that achieved this extraordinary speed was the *A4 Pacific Mallard* built by one of Britain's greatest railway engineers, Sir Nigel Gresley.

The attempt on the record began on the southbound run. *Mallard* had reached an impressive 75 mph by the time she reached Stoke Summit. She then took advantage of the following downhill section and, over the next six miles or so, reached 114 mph, matching the previous record. Soon after that *Mallard* hit 125 mph, before just touching 126 mph for perhaps five seconds.

For the next few miles she never dropped below 120 mph, but the huge stresses and strains on her engine were beginning to tell and, moments later, she dropped to well below 100 mph before returning to Doncaster for repairs.

Mallard was just one of a number of magnificent A4 steam engines built by Gresley in the 1930s for the London and North Eastern Railway. She was not a special train in the sense that she had been built specifically to break speed records – *Mallard* was designed, in fact, simply for passenger carrying, but at a time when different railway companies took enormous pride in achieving ever-higher speeds. *Mallard* was very much a product of the age in which she was built.

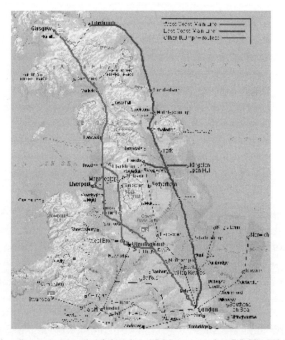

Mallard's greatest rival in the 1930s was the LMS *Silver Link* which had achieved a run of 114 mph earlier in 1938. But *Mallard* had at least one great advantage over all her rivals (apart from the quality of her engineering), namely her aerodynamic shape. Indeed, when he built *Mallard*, Gresley was one of the first railway engineers to recognise the significance of aerodynamics.

The 1930s were the golden years of rail speed – no restrictions were imposed and a driver could go as fast as he was able to make his engine go. Today, after a series of high-profile disasters, speed restrictions are largely imposed because of track conditions. Modern engines are also built to run at speeds less than their maximum theoretical speed in order to reduce wear and tear. In the 1930s such matters were rarely considered and trains could go flat out if the driver and fireman's skills were up to it.

Mallard and the other A4s were never surpassed in terms of their technological brilliance and they continued in service right up until the end of steam in the 1960s.

RAILWAY HERO

ENGLAND, 1941

During the Battle of Britain, Norman Tunna, a Great Western railwayman, was awarded one of Britain's highest awards for an act of extraordinary bravery, but this wasn't bravery on the battlefield – it was bravery on the railway.

It was the night of the first big blitz on Merseyside and, on one huge dock area, 140 men of the Great Western Railway were soon to spend the night battling with the help of outside fire services to save the docks, the ships and their huge stores of cotton, food and munitions.

In the thick of the fires throughout the long night was shunter Norman Tunna. It all began at 7.30pm, when the huge dock area and its scores of railway lines were crowded with wagons and locomotives; shunting engines were going to and fro; trains were being taken apart and then re-made; goods were being discharged and loaded.

Then, through the clear evening sky with no warning, came the low-flying enemy planes. The trains and wagons on the dockyard were sitting targets and among them were dozens of freight wagons loaded with high-explosive shells of all sizes, waiting to be transferred to barges and ships.

Other wagons were packed with tins of petrol and aircraft fuel, flares, daylight bombs, and cordite fuses. Here and there tarpaulins covered huge depth-charges, the most deadly and destructive of all the loads carried by train during the war.

The first bombs the incoming planes dropped were incendiaries – they landed with a tearing sound then crackled and popped like huge fireworks. The railwaymen had been drilled to get into their shelters at the first sign of an attack and this they'd done. But once the bombs began to fall there was a rush to get out of the shelter. Each man, as he came out, picked up one of the sandbags that had been left round the entrance to the shelter and ran in the direction of the fires, now blazing all over the place. Despite the fires and the bombs that continued to rain down the railwaymen could be seen dodging in and out of the railway wagons kicking incendiaries clear.

Then word came through that one of the biggest storage sheds had been hit by incendiaries. Firemen were working on the roof of the shed where huge panes of glass were cracking and exploding but, despite the heat and the danger, the railwaymen rushed into the shed to see if they could get the trains and wagons clear.

The blaze from the shed was now lighting up the whole dock and of course the light from the fire was drawing more planes and more bombs. But amidst the raining bombs, the fires and the explosions, the railwaymen kept working calmly. They seemed to have no thought of danger or personal risk, either on this or on the many nights during which the blitz was to continue.

Then someone realised that a huge ammunition train was up against the side of the blazing shed – it could go up any minute, killing all the men and destroying what was left of the vital railhead. The shedmaster needed shunters but the work was so dangerous he knew he would have to ask for volunteers. Norman Tunna was first to volunteer, then came his mate Edwards. They knew that six trucks, each containing thirty massive, high-explosive bombs, were in imminent danger. Guided by the light from the fires, the two men reached the wagons. Norman Tunna immediately jumped into one of the trucks and began working under the tarpaulin that covered the wagon. This wagon held the very biggest bombs, packed in with strips of wood and already the strips of wood were beginning to burn.

They decided to try to move the burning truck along the rails until it was under the gantry used to load water on to the engines. Tunna climbed aboard the engine and, with the driver, began backing the train away from the burning shed. They were well on the way to a safer line when they had to halt the train at a signal-box while Edwards went to get orders to proceed. Tunna walked the length of the train to see that all was in order, and now for the first time noticed burning debris dropping from one of the high-explosive wagons. He ran back to the engine, got a bucket of water from the injector-pump, and warned the driver not to move. Back again with the water, he scrambled underneath the wagon and then threw the water upwards. This put the fire out under the wagon, but Tunna knew there was still fire inside, under the wagon sheet. To quench this he ran to another signal box for another bucket of water and a stirrup-pump. Norman Tunna recalled what happened next:

I was trying to work the nozzle of the pump under the sheet when Driver Davies and fireman Newns arrived. They'd come in to work for their shift despite the blitz. Climbing on top of the wagon, I found a small hole in the sheet through which the incendiary had made its way. Seeing that it was burning furiously, I decided to throw the whole thing open.

'I'll lift the sheet if you'll undo the ties,' I shouted to Davies and Newns. I gave a good lift to the sheet as soon as they had loosened it, and the three of us turned it back. Flames and smoke streamed out of the wagon. Looking down I could see the wood inside burning fast, and the incendiary, still blazing, jammed between two very big bombs. I made a quick grab for the incendiary, but failed to get it out. It was firmly fixed, and the bombs were getting very hot. Sitting on the side of the wagon I shouted for my shunting pole, thinking to jam it between the bombs, lift one, and so get the incendiary out.

I got the pole in, by the incendiary, but the bombs were too heavy for me. Davies and Newns at once climbed in, caught hold of the pole, and between them levered the two bombs apart. Again I made a grab for the incendiary. This time I had a good hold of it, and threw it away down the line.

That was not quite the end of the truck fire. The wood was still burning and the bombs getting still hotter. So we got the stirrup-pump working and sprayed the bombs and wood until the fire went out. To make matters completely safe we pulled the train under the water column, and gave all the wagons a good soaking.

After putting the ammunition train away safely, Norman Tunna returned to the main fire and continued helping to get other trains out of the area. At daybreak the raid ended. Without his fearless action the ammunition wagon would have certainly exploded, causing untold damage and huge loss of life. He was subsequently awarded the George Cross.

OVER THE JUMPS

ENGLAND, 1942

During the war years railway maintenance was a prime concern because moving goods and men around the country was a vital part of the war effort. However, with the blackout and shortages of men and materials it was very difficult to ensure that the railways were as efficiently run as in peacetime. Risks, inevitably, were taken and accidents happened but it is a tribute to those men in reserved occupations who stayed on the railway throughout hostilities that there were so few accidents. Of course, luck also played a part, as in the extraordinary case of an express train on the Great Western Railway.

It was travelling at more than 60 mph, on its way to the West Country from Paddington, when a connecting rod broke away from the engine and instantly slipped under the train. Passengers later described how the immediate effect was like being on a horse going over jumps. The engine seemed to leap into the air but by a miracle landed perfectly in position back on the tracks when in all honesty it should have been derailed. By a stroke of luck, each and every carriage bounced over the connecting rod and landed full square back on the tracks. The only damage was to the passengers' nerves but it was a one-in-a-million chance that the whole train had not been derailed and, at 60 mph, the consequences might have been too dreadful to contemplate.

DROWNED TRAIN

ENGLAND, 1953

The storms and floods that swept across the Thames Estuary and into Essex, Suffolk and Norfolk in 1953 were the worst ever recorded in Britain. More than three hundred people lost their lives, many from hypothermia after spending a bitterly cold night on the roofs of their houses. Thousands of farm animals were drowned. Along the creeks and estuaries massive surging tides pushed through the streets of villages and dozens of cars and lorries – even pre-fabricated houses – were uprooted and swept away.

At Hunstanton in Norfolk, the 3.20pm for King's Lynn was ready to depart. A gale rocked the train from side to side and rain was driven almost horizontally into the face of the driver and fireman. But they had faced storms before and the heat from their engine would keep them reasonably warm, despite the fact that the footplate on the old locomotive was open to the elements. The train eased out of the station, gathered speed and set off across the flat countryside. Within twenty minutes the driver knew they were in trouble. The floodwaters had come over the rails and all around as far as the eye could see the water was littered with trees, dead animals, crates, boxes and bits of farm equipment.

As darkness fell, the engine hit a bungalow that had been carried on to the tracks. Miraculously the train stayed on the tracks but the locomotive and its firebox were damaged and partially flooded. The train came to a halt and the waters rose ever closer to the windows, where the passengers sat terrified and listening to the howling wind. Almost all the pressure had been lost in the engine, but despite there

315

being no prospect of rescue while conditions worsened by the minute, the fireman had an idea. He peered into the firebox and noticed a few coals still glowing. He fed the tiny fire until he'd created a substantial blaze. After a few quick repairs to the engine pipe-work he managed to raise steam almost to the point where the driver thought they could get the train moving again. Despite the appalling weather, they'd now been standing on the unprotected footplate for several hours. Their fingers were blue with cold but at the first touch of the regulator the train began to move. It inched its way along the track, easing the floating bungalow out of the way and after half a mile or so rose dripping out of the flood and up on to higher ground. Dozens of people aboard that train might easily have died but for the engineering skills of driver and fireman.

FLYING ROD

ENGLAND, 1958

A locomotive is a relatively simple piece of equipment, but it is subject to enormous stresses and strains, particularly when travelling at speed. In fact, given the massive demands made on early steam engines it is amazing that more of them did not either blow up, come off the rails or disintegrate, particularly as so little was then known about metal fatigue and the physics of high-speed travel. Of course, things did still occasionally go wrong and boilers exploded or broke down in various ways right through the steam era. Among the more common causes of breakdown was damage to the connecting rods and on at least one occasion a connecting rod did something quite extraordinary.

It all began when a seaside special set off for one of the most popular resorts on the south coast, packed with children and their parents. The noise of excited children in the cluttered carriages was deafening but their parents were glad to see them enjoying themselves and did little to quieten the tumult.

The train passed through the suburbs at a leisurely pace and then picked up speed as it headed out into the green, early summer countryside. Soon it was passing through villages and market towns before reaching a long straight section of track on which it normally reached its top speed.

The train was probably travelling at nearly 70 miles per hour when the connecting rod snapped off. Amid the noise of the engine and the noise of children playing the sound of it smashing into the ballast at the side of the track went unnoticed, but less than a second

317

later part of it bounced up from the trackside, smashed through one of the compartment windows and, before anyone had time to react or even register what had happened, it crashed out through the plate glass on the other side of the carriage and disappeared. By a million-to-one chance it somehow managed to miss the children jumping and playing about in the compartment. Had it struck one of them there is no question that they would have been instantly killed.

MAGGOT BOX

ENGLAND, 1965

He was a little-known author, the last of that now-vanished species of professional hacks who, given a good brief and a reasonable amount of time, could turn out a good workmanlike book on pretty much any subject. The freelance nature of his work also meant he had plenty of time to pursue his favourite sport, which was fishing. To be absolutely precise he liked fishing the Thames and was often to be found wandering some little-known reach of the river in search of a forgotten backwater or a deep eddy that might contain a 5-pound chub or a 10-pound barbel or even, that most rare thing, a Thames trout.

On this particular day he was travelling to Windsor on the train from Paddington. Usually, he avoided the rush hour period and set off long before most travellers were even out of bed, but on this particular day he'd overslept and was now sitting in a crowded carriage surrounded by smartly dressed businessmen, mothers with their children, students and tourists.

Our fisherman author didn't carry much with him in the way of tackle but he liked to take plenty of bait and on this occasion he had a truly massive bait box filled to the very brim with some of the biggest, liveliest maggots he'd ever seen. The box must have contained at least two gallons of the little larvae.

The train was hot and crowded. The fisherman was tired. He soon fell fast asleep and suddenly, without knowing quite where he was, he was woken by deafening shouts and screams. At first he thought the train must have crashed. All along the carriage men,

319

women and children were jumping about and uttering loud cries of disgust and fear. The fisherman was stunned – or at least he was until he happened to glance down at his tackle bag and bait box. Somehow the bait box had managed to tip over on its side and its lid had come off. Well over half the maggots had spilled on to the carriage floor. While he'd been asleep the motion of the train and the maggots' ceaseless crawling had distributed them evenly over virtually the whole of the carriage from one end to the other.

Thinking he was very likely to be lynched if discovered, our intrepid angler hastily picked up his bits and pieces and made a quick getaway through the connecting door into the next carriage. Having carefully replaced the bait box lid he settled down for a further nap.

THE CARD PLAYERS

CHINA, 1968

The great railway journeys of the world, whether slow mountain climbs in India, remote dusty tracks through South America or the vast spaces of the American west, have earned their reputation largely because of the terrain through which they take their passengers. But for sheer distance and remoteness the greatest railway journey of them all has to be the trans-Siberian railway, which runs for almost six thousand miles across some of the most remote regions of Russia in its journey from Moscow to Bejing.

Day after day spent on this journey can sap the will as the endless, unchanging Russian landscape drifts by. But over the long decades since the railroad was first built the trans-Siberian railroad has witnessed many extraordinary scenes, murders and abductions being almost the commonest. The railway also seems to attract eccentrics, fortune hunters and the dispossessed. Kings and emperors have escaped or gone into exile on the trans-Siberian railway, runaway princesses have eloped on it, but perhaps the most extraordinary event ever to have occurred on it concerned a simple game of snap.

Two elderly Russian businessmen were travelling towards the border with China and to pass the time they played cards. As the days passed they worked their way through every game they knew, but for some reason that no one has ever been able to explain they grew ever more resentful of and angry at each other, to the point at which they were no longer on speaking terms at all – and this despite the fact that they had started their journey as the best of friends.

321

The curiously oppressive nature of the landscape and monotonous motion of the train had clearly had some sinister influence on the two men. Still their endless, almost obsessive games of cards continued. They played every game they could think of until only snap remained, but by now they were playing with deadly seriousness for money and possessions.

Though large sums of money and extravagant promissory notes were involved the balance of wins and losses was pretty even. It was only when they began to play the simplest of all card games – snap – that one of the two elderly men began to lose every single game. He lost again and again and since they were still playing for large sums he grew ever more angry and desperate.

They had kept notes on who owed what to whom but now the loser looked at his list and realised that if this game was ultimately to be taken seriously – and he feared that would be the case – then he had lost everything. His opponent was beginning to refuse to play any further games on the grounds that his opponent had nothing left to bet or at least could not match the largest bets. When he discovered that his partner meant to take everything owed to him when they returned to Moscow he became desperate and just a few dozen miles from the Chinese border he lost his last game, pulled out a pistol and shot his former friend dead. He then pushed the body out of the train and hid all the evidence of his existence on the train and their card game. But he forgot one thing. The Russians had been so paranoid about being invaded that they took precautions during the Stalinist era to make sure that invasion by train was impossible by making sure their track gauge was different from everyone else's. This meant that no Polish or Chinese train could run into Russia.

To ensure that a train service could run in and out of their country despite the fact that their gauge was different from everyone else's the Russians agreed a special procedure with several of their neighbour countries. When a train arrived at a border crossing, its carriages would be lifted off their bogies – their wheels – and then new bogies would be run underneath them and the carriages lowered once again into position. The passengers didn't even leave their compartments while this bizarre procedure was carried out, but with bogies changed, the train could continue on its way on the new gauge.

Unfortunately for the elderly card player, bits of his former friend were found attached to the bogy underneath his carriage when the train finally reached the Chinese border and he was promptly arrested.

GHOST TRAIN

ENGLAND, 1973

East Anglia suffered more than most parts of the UK from the infamous Dr Beeching's cuts. The devastation he caused to the rail network left abandoned stationhouses, embankments and bridges all over Suffolk and Norfolk. Many of the old station houses were eventually sold to families who live in them to this day, but the tracks were ripped up, the bridges crumbled away and rabbits colonised the embankments.

The old branch lines that passed lonely isolated villages had never been hugely popular but for locals who did not have cars and, for the elderly, the trains that passed through each day made getting to the nearest big town a pleasure. Then one day the trains stopped forever and an eerie silence fell along the tracks. Grass and weeds grew up around the sleepers and the rails began to rust. But long after the trains were no more, many local people still heard or thought they heard the sounds of trains rattling across the countryside.

Even the local newspapers carried occasional stories about these ghost trains and a psychic was called in by one editor to try to discover if there really was any substance to the stories beyond the dreams and midnight imaginings of the local people.

The psychic wandered the deserted embankments late into the night and used odd little electric boxes of his own devising to see if he could detect anything. At first there was nothing. But then three days into the job he had settled down by the side of the track, with his little box of tricks purring and clicking beside him, when he heard the unmistakable breathing sound of a steam locomotive. He thought for a moment he must have fallen asleep, so distinct was the sound, but on looking up he saw quite clearly the outline of a train coming towards him. It was a long way off still, but the shape and noise were unmistakable.

Then something even more extraordinary happened. There was a huge bang, the distant image of the train became confused and then the psychic heard screams. Seconds later he saw the outline of flames flickering high into the sky. Instinct took over and he ran towards the flames. He ran till he thought his lungs would burst, but, glancing down for a split second, noticed what he had known all along – there were no rails. There could be no train. He stopped and, desperately trying to get his breath back, kicked a few of the remaining bits of ballast that lay about. He looked up again in the direction of the flames and saw nothing. The inky sky was still but for the faint outline of a moving cloud and all around was silence. No flames, no screams, no train. He wandered on for more than a mile but there was nothing.

When he made his report the next day to the newspaper editor he explained what he had seen but could offer no explanation for it. He returned to London and as the weeks passed began to think that he must after all have nodded off and in his heightened state of expectation imagined everything. Six months passed and then one morning he received a letter. It was written in an almost illegible hand with no address. The writer explained that he was now in his nineties and had seen the psychic's report on his night on the disused railway. The old man went on to explain how sixty years earlier several people had been killed in a train smash at exactly the spot the psychic had described.

OH BROTHER

SWEDEN, 1980

Like most sports, fishing has its share of apocryphal stories. Occasionally, such stories have the ring of truth about them. One such is told regularly to visitors to Swedish Lapland. In the more remote parts of this extremely cold and extremely isolated region, well within the Arctic Circle, live a number of men, mainly Lapps, who find the solitude very much to their liking. In some instances elderly Lapps can be found in unheated log cabins more than fifty miles from the nearest village or other settlement.

One man, who was probably in his seventies at the time, made his living by catching and selling the prolific grayling of the region. He went for months at a time without seeing or speaking to another human being, but he had lived in his isolated hut for many years, perfectly happily, and got about on a snow-mobile, visiting the nearest town just once or twice a year for essential supplies.

The old Lapp had two brothers who were even older than he was – one probably in his late seventies, the other almost certainly more than eighty. Each brother lived a similar life but many miles from each other in the almost permanently frozen landscape. Then tragedy struck. The eldest brother died one terrible winter. His two brothers met to decide what to do. The weather made any idea of taking the body to the nearest town for burial out of the question, so the two brothers decided to keep the corpse on ice, as it were, until the spring, when it could be disposed of properly.

The body of their eldest brother was duly left in a shallow grave in the ice. As soon as the weather eased, the two brothers dug up

326

their brother, loaded him on to a snowmobile and set off for a small railway station some thirty miles away.

The train would be quicker and more convenient than any attempt to take the body by snowmobile all the way to the town, but there was a problem. The train only took passengers. It didn't even have a guard's van. But the brothers, practical and unsentimental about such things, decided they could get round the problem if they sat their dead, and very well-preserved, brother propped up between them. He'd been kept in his suit since the day he died and if anyone noticed anything untoward the brothers would simply say he was ill and asleep. Besides, the town was only an hour by train and they had arranged to be met by more suitable transport at the other end.

Duly arrived at the station, the two brothers wedged the dead man between them and got him into a compartment without too much difficulty. Once on board the brothers relaxed. There were hardly any other passengers travelling that day and they had only an hour to kill.

The two brothers had hardly ever been on a train and after a while they decided they would go and look at the buffet car and perhaps buy themselves a warming drink. Certain that the next stop (half an hour away) was theirs, they were quite happy to leave their dead brother propped up in his corner. They set off for the buffet car, but they were mistaken about the train. It had one more stop to make before it reached the town and when it stopped there ten minutes later a man struggled aboard with a very heavy suitcase. He dragged it into the first compartment he could find, which happened to be where the dead brother sat leaning and apparently fast asleep in the corner.

The traveller decided that rather than leave his heavy suitcase on the floor of the carriage he would try to lift it into one of the luggage racks. Despite its great weight he'd almost lifted it into position when the train lurched, he lost his grip and the suitcase crashed down on to the sleeping passenger. Horrified, the traveller mumbled his apologies and lifted his suitcase off the elderly man, who'd been knocked to the floor by the force of the blow. When he tried to help the old man back into his seat he realised with horror that the old man was dead. The old man must have been very frail for the weight of the suitcase had certainly killed him. The traveller panicked and decided there was just one thing to do: he dragged the old man to the door, opened it and pushed him out into the snowy darkness.

Two minutes later the traveller was back in the compartment trying to compose himself when the two brothers returned from the buffet car.

'Where on earth is our brother?' they asked.

'Oh him,' came the reply, 'he got off at the last stop.'

History does not record the reactions of the two brothers but the story has a happy ending. When the traveller was told that the old man had been dead all along he confessed to his part in the old man's disappearance. The body was recovered the next day and the old man's funeral went ahead as planned the following week.

THE LAST OIL LAMPS

ENGLAND, 1998

A traveller on a Somerset line was astonished as his train entered the station at Yeovil Pen Mill to see that the semaphore signals were lit by oil lamps. He thought he must be dreaming but on making enquiries discovered that every week since the station had opened in 1857 a railwayman had topped up the 24 lamps with paraffin and trimmed their wicks.

The oil lamps had long outlasted the steam era and British Railways simply because, like much of the so-called old technology of the steam era, they were well designed and did their job efficiently. But in the end, efficiency alone was not enough to save them and this last link with the early railway gave way at last to twentieth-century technology.